2—

D1499678

WITHDRAWN

BESSIE
YELLOWHAIR

Books by Grace Halsell

BESSIE YELLOWHAIR

BLACK/WHITE SEX

SOUL SISTER

PERU

With Charles Evers

EVERS: CHARLES EVERS' FRANK AUTOBIOGRAPHY

BESSIE YELLOWHAIR

by Grace Halsell

William Morrow & Company, Inc.
New York   1973

Printed in the United States of America.
Library of Congress Catalog Card Number 73-9378

ISBN 0-688-0020-5

1 2 3 4 5 77 76 75 74 73

Contents

Prologue 9

PART I THE BEGINNING 13

PART II ON THE RESERVATION 39

PART III BESSIE YELLOWHAIR 121

Epilogue 210

Prologue

Washington, D. C.
June, 1973

It is only a few hundred miles from an isolated, dirt-floored hut made of mud and sticks on the barren Navajo reservation to the complacent suburbs of Orange County, California. But the distance cannot be truly measured in miles. It is a leap from primitive tranquillity to modern tumult and tensions, overabundance and pollution, hypocrisy and prejudices.

When I left the reservation, I had no identification, no credit cards, driver's license, checkbook—nothing to identify me except the Indian clothes that I wore and the Indian name that I bore and what I had come to feel, psychologically.

I had adopted the role of an "Indian" to learn what life would be like for a Navajo in a middle-class white environment. The experience was brief but suffocating. It was demeaning and traumatic. It took a powerful exercise of will for me to summon the strength to run in the night, to end my masquerade and my anguish. It was a chilling nightmare, a helpless cry in the dark, a moment of self-degradation.

Back in Washington, depleted, confused, ill, I told a friend I had "run away" from my experience as an "Indian" domestic.

"I'm disappointed in you," my friend said. "You never *ran* from being 'black.' "

9

But wasn't there a difference? As a "black" I was like any other tough-minded, competitive, aggressive American.

But as an "Indian," I was submissive, passive, and extremely vulnerable, not knowing how to defend myself against the more subtle oppression of an almost impersonal "enemy," contemptuous, arrogant, insensitive.

I could entertain but two alternatives: remain "Indian" and atrophy, or run in the night. I ran.

And even after I escaped back into the white world, I felt the agony of emotions in conflict: my values, aspirations, mode of life seemed somehow to be under indictment. Through a transference I hardly understood, I believed that the Indian concept of *being* was more appealing than that of achieving.

I went to my doctor and lay on his examination table, and he massaged my liver. "Does that hurt? Where does it hurt?" he asked.

I wanted to say what the Navajos say—*Tah honeesgai,* I feel bad all over.

"You are jaundiced," the doctor told me. And added I must be hospitalized for infectious hepatitis.

But instead I returned to my mother's home in Texas, and to the same bed where in 1970 I had recovered from serum hepatitis, contracted in a modern hospital. Lying on a dirt floor or in a $100-a-day Anglo hospital, you can fall sick from the same virus. My mind conjured up other odd patterns. *Now why was I sick?* The reservation was without medicine cabinets filled with nostrums, to be sure. Some of the water used for drinking was contaminated; my resistance had declined under the rigors of primitive living. But weren't there other reasons? While illnesses have their own special sources, *something else* helps cause them. That something else, difficult to name, is not a germ.

Had not my difficulty in coping with two worlds—Indian and white—contributed to my illness?

Again I had learned a lesson in human limitations. We have only so much energy, so much tolerance for stress.

Weeks later, I lunched with a friend and told him I found life among the Navajos difficult. "That's because of what your forefathers did to them," he said.

No, no, I protested. My heart isn't bleeding for humanity and I'm not guilt-stained because of what my father did to the Indians. Rather it is the burden of my values, rules, judgments.

When I went to live among the Navajos in early 1972, I packed very lightly, but felt weighted down with my own values and conceits.

Being a product of a uniquely modern country without roots in its own continental past and with cultural traditions brought from Europe, I tend to view life "rationally," as a cause-and-effect phenomenon, supported by rationales and logic. The Indians, who came here from China and Tibet, on the other hand, have a different heritage and approach life instinctively or intuitively.

In our "discovery" of the New World, we treated the Indians as obstacles to be overcome or subjugated, not human beings to be understood. They were offered two choices: yield to our dominance or perish. The tyranny was total, and now after centuries of lordly domination, not even a belated sense of guilt and contrition has produced the understanding that is essential to all human relationship. The Indians are still misunderstood.

I determined to live as an Indian among the Navajos, and then to "pass" as a Navajo among whites.

But I did not feel inside me that I was Indian, or even that I could be. How could I step into an Indian's shoes, much less into an Indian's mind?

I met an Indian woman, Bessie Yellowhair, and after we became friends, I asked if I might borrow her clothes, her name, her identity. I would try to convey her attitudes and outlook toward white America, or the *Anglos,* as she would put it. And she gave me my greatest compliment, "Of course, Grace, *you are like a sister.*" This book bears Bessie Yellowhair's name because she is my sister, too, her life insinuated into mine unforgettably.

My interest in Indians was acquired, of course. But, in a very real way, it was also inherited. It began with my father. . . .

Part I

THE BEGINNING

Had my father lived he would be 112 years old today; I say *had he lived,* and yet in a sense he lives for me. When he died on February 4, 1957, *The New York Times* headlined his obituary:

> "Harry H. Halsell, 96
> Indian Fighter
> Texas Rancher Who Once
> Outfoxed Geronimo Dies—
> Was Author of 9 Books"

The *Times* story related that he had his own six-shooter when he was seven, was on the trail driving longhorns to northern markets when he was eleven. And the story continued:

> On several occasions Mr. Halsell used his six-guns and rifle to ward off Indians.
> Mr. Halsell said one of his closest scrapes came on Christmas Eve, 1880, in Southwestern New Mexico.
> He had driven his stock into a small valley with only one entrance and bedded them down. Near midnight, in the moonlight, he spotted a group of Apaches riding toward him.
> Mr. Halsell said he mounted his horse, held the reins in his teeth and fired a six-gun in each hand as he charged the group.
> The Indians, believing a large band was attacking them, scattered and Mr. Halsell escaped. He said he

later learned the feared Geronimo had been in the lead and the band had just ambushed a stagecoach.

In my father's day, the land of the Navajos lay in the middle of a dark continent. When he "outfoxed" Geronimo, in the incident *The New York Times* story relates, he was guarding stock that was owned by the Santa Fe railway, then laying its tracks on the southern fringe of Navajoland.

Today I study the *Times* headline—"Indian Fighter." His being a "fighter" and outfoxing Geronimo plainly were more important than his writing books. And I wonder about the nature of man, all men, that they honor their fighters above their poets. Genghis Khan, Alexander, Caesar, Napoleon come more readily to mind than do the poets and philosophers of their times.

When I was a small child, I toddled to my father's lap and said, "Let me paint your face like an Indian's." He put down the newspaper he was reading and I plaited his long white hair and powdered his face and rouged his cheeks, and when I was finished I put a mirror to his face. He said, "You did a mighty fine job."

"Talk Indian, Daddy," I said.

And I listened to his Indian talk, a gibberish of sounds that I never asked to be translated because my childish mind supplied its own translation. I did not think in words; rather in images, and not even explicit images. I always thought of wind—wild gusts of wind—that seemed also to talk Indian talk and to convey their own images and to be not wind at all but a very lonely person.

When I was four and five years old my father terrified me with stories drawn from his own childhood when he was being chased by Indians on the Texas frontier. They were always "wild," and boy and man had to be stout of heart and comfortable with their firearms to survive.

Nearly every aspect of life was dominated by fear of Indians. For instance, when my father's father built his frontier home, using straight, strong oak logs and sand and lime mortar, he designed it "so it would be hard to set fire to by the Indians."

Once my father's mother sent him and his brother Oscar up Martin's Creek in Wise County to their grandmother's house to get some flour. As my father related it, the two boys were returning home when Oscar looked to the west and hollered out:

" 'Look at the Indians! Follow me!'

"I saw a sight that chilled my blood. The woods, not sixty yards away, seemed full of painted warriors. The Indians figured we could make a run in the open field, and that would have been easy picking for them. But they had to deal with Oscar, one of the bravest and most level-headed boys that ever lived. Instead of making a run in the open for Grandma's house or crossing into the open field on the east side, my brother made a run for a dense thicket, a little in the direction of the Indians. He knew the pig trails in this thicket, and it being almost dark, the Indians could not find us."

In my father's stories I always saw a vast expanse of trackless prairie and tall sage dancing with the wild grace of an improvised ballet. I saw rivers overflowing their banks and on bright, moonshiny nights "savage" Indians riding over the hill, screaming and hollering on their paint ponies.

Indians rode and rampaged through my childhood memories, fed by my father's inexhaustible tales and descriptions. His stories were not fantasies concocted by a doting parent to titillate his children, but very real. My father's youth and young manhood were lived during the most turbulent years of the white man's struggle to overpower, if not destroy, the red man.

The Comanche and the Kiowa, called by my father "the most cruel and bloodthirsty of all barbarous tribes of Indians in Texas history," fought a losing fight, but they often took a heavy toll for their revenge. My father relates:

"In 1865, the Indians made a raid in Wise County and carried off two Babb children, Bianca, a girl, and J. E. (Dot), a boy. These children were small when carried away. Three years afterward a trapper was selling his pelts in the settlements and was telling about seeing a white boy and girl with the Comanches. Old Mr. Babb heard the tale and arranged to buy the children. The deal was made and the children brought home but they had adopted Indian ways and habits."

What were those Indian ways and habits? Only now, years and years after I first heard the story, do I really begin to wonder, to want to know.

Soon after the Babb children were kidnapped, the Apaches abducted Herman Lehmann, eleven, during a raid on his family's Texas farm, and the boy became the adopted son of Comanche chief Quanah Parker. When the whites and the Comanches made peace, Chief Parker persuaded Lehmann to rejoin his family, but the young man had forgotten English and he later wrote, ". . . I knew that I had found my people. But I was an Indian, and I did not like the whites because they were palefaces. And I wanted immediately to go back to the tribe."

On June 21, 1866, my father's uncle George Halsell, a line rider on the 10,000-acre Dan Waggoner ranch, was killed by Indians, thirteen miles southwest of Henrietta, Texas. My father later recalled:

"As George Halsell and Pete Harding were coming down Lake Creek late in the evening they stopped to water their horses. Just between them and the brush was a small hill, and the cowboys' backs were toward this hill. Suddenly, there came over the hill a yelling band of Comanche Indians.

"George had a fast horse and Pete a slow horse, and George held his horse back, firing on the Comanches and allowing Pete to escape. But while George was firing with his six-shooter one Indian got close to him and shot him in the back with a rifle and broke his backbone. He then ran full speed toward the high prairie and his horse attempted to leap across a wide ditch, but failed to make it and fell backward into the ditch. The Indians then came up and killed and scalped him."

My father, in looking back over his Indian wars, realized that he and other white men lived by that "good old plan . . . that they should take who have the power, and they should keep who can!" At the time of his death, a Texas newspaper recalled a story of my father's driving cattle to a northern market when he was stopped by Chief Quanah Parker.

"You big chief?" Chief Parker asked. "Cattle eat my grass—want 30 beeves."

Halsell, who with 15 cowboys was driving a herd of 3,000 longhorns 15 miles southwest of the Wichita Mountains near Fort Sill in Oklahoma, said, "Vamoose, *tiene nada*" [Get out, you get nothing].

The Indian chief waved a blanket and more than 30 redskins appeared out of the bushes. With the yelling Indians getting closer Halsell offered the chief one cow and no more.

The chief, with arms folded, stood still and silent for a moment. Finally the chief spoke:

"Me take cow."

Halsell drew a sigh of relief.

In recalling that scene, my father once told me:

"When I met Quanah Parker he was a very fine-looking young chief—stood straight and was six feet tall. Our meeting near the Wichita Mountains was not very friendly. In later years he and I became friends and hunted in the breaks and mountains of King County, Texas.

"One day when we were hunting big game he said, 'Halsell, I want you to write a letter to President Roosevelt.' I got a pencil and paper and said, 'I'm ready to go.' Then he dictated this letter to Theodore Roosevelt:

"'Mr. Roosevelt: The same day that I saw that you had killed a buck in the Dallas *News*, I killed two bucks at the Burk Burnett's ranch.'

"I said, 'All right, what next?' His answer was, 'That's all.'

"I mailed the letter and in ten days this letter came from Teddy Roosevelt:

"'Dear Quanah: I received your letter, and was very much amused.'"

My father said: "The story indicates Parker's penchant for brevity and irony; he was indicating that the white man Roosevelt had killed his deer *only on paper*, while he himself had in fact killed two live ones."

When I was fourteen and my father was seventy-seven, he took me out of school to drive the car for him as he traveled around Texas selling his book *Cowboys and Cattleland*, relating "the true story of a wild and rugged frontier life full of daring deeds and wild adventures . . . up to a period of cultured, well-settled society."

We drove along the Chisholm Trail named, he told me, "for a half-breed Indian, Jesse Chisholm." And only now do I wonder: Why does one say half-breed Indian when one never says half-breed white?

In his stories dealing with his childhood—when the collective urge was to subdue or annihilate the Indian—my father painted broad canvases of menace, terming the red man "savage," "wild," "bloodthirsty," "barbarous." But when he was in his late forties he gave away his fortune in cattle and land. As he put it, "All of my life I had been interested in cows; then I got interested in people, in their *souls.*" He began to read, reflect, and to contemplate the wholeness of life, with its harmonies and discords.

When my father was eighty-six we drove from Fort Worth, where we were then living, north to Decatur in Wise County, where he was born.

"I want to find Bianca Babb, who was kidnapped by the Comanche in 1865," he told me.

Typical of so many young people, I was interested in the *present* moment, and his stories about the Indians seemed more ancient than the rocks. In Decatur, we found the house where the old white-haired woman—the same age as my father—lived. I sat in the car, and watched my father walk briskly to the door, and I saw Bianca Babb come out on the front porch, and saw the two of them sit in a porch swing, discussing the Comanche raid of so long ago.

On the way back to Fort Worth, my father talked again about the terror he had known as a child, fearing that the Indians would raid the small white settlement and kidnap him.

He said whenever a white was kidnapped settlers embarked on expeditions to bring him back. Always there was the question: can the prisoner, if located, be rehabilitated? And the feeling that the white inhabitants had a tenuous grasp upon their own culture.

My father told me, "Bianca Babb recalls only 'good' days, and 'good' treatment with the Comanches."

Then he was silent for a while; and he reflected that "our" stories had always concerned the white people who had been scalped by the Indians, "but what we don't admit is that this practice was taught the American Indians by the whites—who offered a bounty for every Indian scalp taken.

"In frontier days, white men took Indian scalps with as little compunction as the Indians took ours. Scalping, denounced as Indian savagery, was actually spread by whites. Governor Kieft of New Amsterdam is credited with the first payments for Indian scalps. And this practice effectively killed off the Indians in New Jersey and New York.

"The Indian was called barbarous, and the Comanches did scalp white people, fasten their scalps to their belts, and go to war dances with these scalps, but I have seen white people in Wise County at picnics exhibiting Indian scalps as trophies of conquests, and some of these scalps were from Indian women. I criticized this gruesome practice one time at a reunion, and that put a stop to it."

In his memoirs, my father wrote:

Of course there was internecine war between the frontier white people and Indians. There were also causes for this strife. And the unthinking, highly prejudiced, superficially minded element of the white people always looked upon Lo [the poor Indian] as the aggressor and called him savage. There lurked in the minds of the early white settlers of America a desire to push out and carve out for themselves a fortune and a home in the new land.

They were willing to make the adventure, take the risk, because of their dream of the future. The Indian was the original owner of the land; and while agriculture and the civilizing influences of orderly society had little appeal to his rugged nature, yet it was his hunting ground. Although he knew little and cared less for the white man's ways, he did realize his vast hunting grounds were being taken away from him. When anyone familiar with the customs and habits of English landlords in the care and love of their vast hunting lodges will reflect, they will recall the brutal treatment meted out to anyone found trespassing on the same lord's hunting ground, and they will understand and appreciate why the Indian resented the encroachment of an alien race on his native land.

The strife could have been amicably settled if the white race had been willing to barter for it fairly. But greed predominated, and they went at the venture like Rob Roy, whose motto was, "The good old plan it sufficeth them, that he should take who had the power, and he should keep who can." This reminded me of the Texas cowman's law; the six-shooter and Winchester were the sovereign arbiters of all disputes.

One beautiful day I was riding up the Cimarron River bottom and was about one-half mile from the north bank. On the north bank were some high sand hills covered with Chinaberry trees. There was a lone Indian standing on top of this sand hill with folded arms and erect figure. He stood for a long time, silent and alone, gazing off down the meandering course of the river.

It was a quiet, beautiful summer day; as far as the eye could see there were clumps of trees, beautiful valleys, with now and then a bunch of cattle either grazing out in the valleys or lying in the shade of cottonwood trees. I was concealed, and while he could not see me I was watching him. I knew he was dreaming but could not interpret his dream. It may have been he was enjoying the pleasant scene. It may have been he was dreaming of past glories, of the once happy hunting grounds now disturbed by the encroachment of the cowman and soon to be settled by the farmer.

Then I reflected on the difference between that lone Indian with his sentiments and memories and the cold, calculating white man who possesses no ideals or dreams above the gratification of his animal passions and his desire for power. While that lone Indian was dreaming, I was dreaming dreams and seeing visions. I not only saw in visions vanishing races of the American Indian, but I saw the long line of Aztecs in Mexico vanish before the conquering soldiers of Spain under Cortes and his successors. I saw in unending centuries weaker races go down and vanish before stronger tribes, all of which seemed to encourage the idea of the survival of the fittest.

As a child, listening to my father's Indian stories, I heard and in one sense saw, smelled and felt, almost tasted the past that he had lived through. While I might have imagined the herds of buffalo, so many that they couldn't be counted, I could not actually "hear" the shrill ping of the rifle shot fired by the buffalo killer who took the tongue and hide and left the carcass for carrions to eat. I might have visualized the herds of longhorns trailing north, but my father still had the dust in his nostrils, he still listened for the echo of the bawling calves, and the thunder of the stampedes.

My father was born in the year the first Pony Express left St. Joseph, Missouri, and, ten days later, delivered letters in Sacramento, California. He saw the first train that came into Texas, sent one of the first telegrams, talked on one of the first telephones, turned on one of the first electric lights this country ever had. His years spanned the Civil War to the atomic bomb, from our sixteenth President, Abraham Lincoln, to our thirty-fourth President, Dwight D. Eisenhower. When he was in his seventies, eighties and nineties, he would reflect on how the country had looked—before there were any fences. In those days the grass was always tall, the rivers were always overflowing their banks. The transitions he witnessed

—fences, pavement, towns and cities, electricity—were so easily defined as progress, civilization.

To advance, to "civilize," was Christian, it was *moral.* Long before my father's time, a papal bull issued to Spanish and Portuguese rulers had proclaimed the "Doctrine of Discovery"—which meant, simply, that a Christian nation (i.e., populated by whites) had the right to claim non-Christian lands (i.e., populated by Indians). In the years that followed, Christians announced their "manifest destiny," meaning that all who were not Christian must get right, or get out of the way.

My father and other "brave, fearless" cowboys, assuming the moral persuasion of the typical homesteader, saw their triumph over the "savages" as inevitable, foreordained, divinely blessed. It was their Christian duty to take the land, square it off, settle it—and push the Indians back if not completely annihilate them. The Indians won an occasional skirmish, but victory for the whites was a foregone conclusion. The whites outnumbered the Indians, held vast stores of ammunition and had long years of experience in organized killings.

The whites always claimed they wanted to save the Indians' souls; but the Indians soon learned it was their soil they wanted.

Emerich de Vattel, an eighteenth-century Swiss jurist, wrote a classic justification for the actions of European settlers throughout the world:

"The whole earth is destined to furnish sustenance for its inhabitants; but it can not do this unless it be cultivated. Every nation is therefore bound by the natural law to cultivate the land which has fallen to its share, and it has no right to extend its boundaries or to obtain help from other nations except in so far as the land it inhabits can not supply its needs . . .

"Those who still pursue this idle [i.e., hunting] mode of life occupy more land than they would have need of under a system of honest labor, and they may not complain if other more industrious nations, too confined at home, should come and occupy part of their lands. Thus, while the conquest of the civilized Empires of Peru and Mexico was a notorious usurpation, the establishment of various colonies upon the continent of North America might, if done within just limits, have been entirely lawful. The peoples of those vast tracts of land rather roamed over them than inhabited them."

Writing in the 1830's, de Tocqueville noted that "the Georgians, who are so much annoyed by the proximity of the Indians, inhabit a territory which does not at present contain more than seven inhabitants to the square mile. In France there are one hundred and sixty-two inhabitants to the same extent of country." He had added that "from whichever side we consider the destinies of the aborigines of North America, their calamities appear to be irremediable; if they continue barbarous, they are forced to retire; if they attempt to civilize their manners, the contact of a more civilized community subjects them to oppression and destitution. They perish if they continue to wander from waste to waste, and if they attempt to settle they still must perish."

Even in our so-called more enlightened day, there must be many people who would agree with an opinion expressed by John Wayne, who spent much of his life fighting Indians on the screen: "I don't feel we did wrong in taking this great country away from them. There were great numbers of people who needed new land, and the Indians were selfishly trying to keep it for themselves."

Our heroes are always, it seems, those who kill, not the slain, not the peaceful ones who want to live in harmony with nature. I recall going with my father to the grave of

Buffalo Bill in Colorado. My father had once heard William Frederick (Buffalo Bill) Cody openly boast, "I killed 4,280 buffalos during a period of less than eighteen months." On another occasion, Cody had said, "I always admired General Custer as a man and an officer. I have often wished I might have been with him at Little Big Horn."

I correspond almost daily with my brother, Ed—Oscar Edward—who also was greatly influenced by the stories our father told us about Indians.

From 1968 to 1970, Ed worked for the Navajo tribal judges in Arizona as their legal adviser. He advised the Indians mostly on how to deal with the U.S. Government, and they paid him for his legal services.

Once, while he was still on the reservation, I made a hurried trip to see him and his wife Betty. Ed drove me over portions of the reservation that encompasses a huge chunk of Arizona, as well as parts of New Mexico and Utah.

Navajoland, he told me, "extends about three hundred miles, just west of Albuquerque to the Grand Canyon; and about one hundred and fifty miles from south to north."

A child of the "jet age," I asked about the nearest airports. "There aren't any *nearest*—he smiled—"but you can think about Salt Lake City or Denver to the north, Las Vegas or Los Angeles to the west, Albuquerque to the east, and Phoenix to the south."

And he gave me other nuggets of information:

—The Navajo is the largest tribe in the United States, with 130,000 members. And Navajoland, the largest of the Indian reservations, comprises almost as much land as the states of Vermont, New Hampshire, Connecticut and Rhode Island, combined.

—The Navajo tribe is unique not only in size, but also in

diversity: the sixteen-million-acre reservation is part desert, part forest, interspersed with deposits of coal, oil, uranium and other minerals.

—Although collectively among the richest Indians, individually the Navajo rank among the poorest.

—The average per capita income of the Navajo living on the reservation is $1,000 per annum, compared with a national average of about $4,000 a year.

—Anglos transformed the tribe from one of the most self-sufficient into one of the most dependent of human communities.

I asked: but weren't our policies changing? Our officials becoming more enlightened?

Ed said that while our government spends about one-half billion dollars annually on Indian programs, whites administer those programs and usually end up with the money; thus Washington's policies have not benefited the Indians. He emphasized several sad facts of their lives:

—Education: drop-out rates for Indians are twice the national averages. The average Indian educational level is less than six years of school.

—Unemployment: as high as 80 percent on some reservations, and exceeding 50 percent among the Navajo labor force.

—Health: it lags twenty-five years behind the general population. Average age at death is forty-four. The infant mortality rate is about 50 percent higher among Indians than it is for the general population.

His figures were all so depressing. I asked what *his* answer was.

"We must begin by admitting that Anglo policies have failed; that the non-Indian doesn't know what's best for the Indian. The Navajos, for example, should be in charge of their reservation. And the Navajo judges and police should have jurisdiction over non-Indians on the reservation. Indians want the political and economic power to run their own lives in their own way."

In 1970, after finishing his stint as legal adviser to the Navajo judges, Ed moved to Houston, where he practices law. But he still had a keen interest in the Navajos, and he urged me to visit them as soon as possible. "You need to go live among them," he wrote.

"Regarding your health: You will be better off on the reservation: regularity, clean air, calm, beauty, peace, safety—you will be better off there than with all that doctors and pills can do! The climate is *desert*. Therefore you can expect dry beautiful days with warm mid-afternoon temperatures, but very cold nights and early mornings. Two or three times during the winter a storm will come through and leave two or three inches of snow. It will melt in two to five days to mud. Then roads, other than a few paved ones, become impassable except for four-wheel drive vehicles and a few skillfully operated pickups. But *most* of the time it is dry.

"You will want a good map. You should first drive all over to get the feel of the reservation."

At the Library of Congress I buried myself in a mound of books written by anthropologists and sociologists who go to reservations with their measuring devices, charts, and probing, numerical queries. It was the Indian authority Vine Deloria who remarked sardonically that every Indian family has its house anthropologist. White experts on Indians place the red man under magnifying glass or into scientific test tubes, and endlessly weigh, measure, card-index and examine him. The trend toward computerizing people has, it seems to me, turned the human heart into data for an IBM machine and lost in the process much precious understanding. We have now studied the Indian almost out of existence.

When my friend Roscoe Dixon comes by for a coffee I tell him I plan to go among the Indians, to live as they live, on the ground, under the stars, in their sparse mud huts. Just simply "turn Indian." Momentarily placing himself in my shoes, he says:

"I wouldn't know where to begin."

I plan to fly to Albuquerque, rent a Volkswagen.

"Why one of those bugs?" he asks.

Because, I explain, the windswept Navajo terrain is extremely rugged; some families live fifty miles from the nearest improved road and one needs extra traction to maneuver through the sand and gullies and over rocky, mountain paths.

My family and friends wholeheartedly approve of my going to live among the Indians. It is almost as if I will be lifting myself, socially, by associating with a "pure, noble breed."

It was different when I set forth as a "black," for a book, entitled *Soul Sister*, portraying how a black woman fares in white America. After that experience, I heard a persistent question: "Why would you want to do that?" There was an undertone of condemnation, a hint that I had somehow degraded myself in a socially unacceptable manner. The insinuation lingered that I had even committed a breach of morality living among the blacks.

Once, at Southern Methodist University, after I had lectured on my *Soul Sister* experiences, an angry white male student accosted me: he was "sure" I had turned myself "black" because I desired a black man.

No one imputes sexual motives to the sandaled long-hairs who choose to do social work among the Navajos, as so often happens when young whites go to live and work among the blacks. No white ever concerns himself with red sex; or red/white sex. Whatever it is or isn't, we are all rather sure that it's quite normal. Have we traditionally seen "black" and "red" Americans as different species?

I board a luxuriously appointed TWA airliner with its piped-in music and bright, attentive stewardesses. I am on my way to Albuquerque. A businessman takes the seat next to mine, and comments on the weather. In my new life I no longer will hear the chatter of "friendly" people who want to "communicate." Now I want to learn to be quiet, passive, receptive, a vessel for all that the Navajos have to teach me. I want to be more than a professional journalist observing and writing with detachment. I want to immerse myself in Navajo ways, customs, attitudes. Travel to learn, my father urged, not to teach.

We land in Chicago, in a blinding snowstorm; we are delayed for an hour. Then the plane lifts up into the clouds, above the blizzard and the pollution, into celestial sunshine. For me it is always a homecoming to return to the world of space, to a realm that stretches out like the vastness of the sea, and provides a more mystical beauty than one finds in sonnets and sonatas. Below I look to a world that we are told is overpopulated, eroded, over-grazed. Yet how pristine, virgin, *empty* it looks!

Often in travel I have experienced a sense of discovery when looking out on a scene so verdant and fresh I seemed to have caught nature in the act of achieving her creation. When I stood on top of the "lost" Inca citadel at Machu Picchu, I thought about Hiram Bingham who had "discovered" it, and when I sailed down the Amazon I thought about Orellana who had "discovered" that mighty ocean sea. And yet before them, there were the thousands of

Indians who built the "lost" city and thousands of Indians who for centuries had lived along the banks of the Amazon.

Now, gazing down to the "emptiness" of the land, I try to see it as the first people in this New World might have seen it. For their eyes were indeed the first human eyes ever to behold the wonders of this continent. They, a people with a yellowish, not a reddish, tinge to their skin and with slanted eyes, really "discovered" America.

They did not come by boat or by horseback or by any conveyances on wheels. They were all walking—from China and Tibet—a distance that we can't imagine traversing, except as we do today, by jet. They started from northern Asia and crossed over a land bridge to Alaska at the end of the last glacial period. Parents died; their children continued the trek. How long ago did their journey begin? No one can say for sure, but it was twenty thousand or more years ago. Several independent groups made the migration, and through the ensuing millennia they kept coming, gradually pushing down into Central and South America.

Since we've never found evidence of prehuman anthropoid species anywhere in the New World, the Asian immigrants must have been the first people ever to inhabit this land. All Americans, then, including the Indians and the Eskimos, are descendants of immigrants. The Indians were here to greet Columbus and the Spaniards, but no one was here to greet the Indians. They truly saw it as it must have looked in the beginning.

Scientific evidence indicates that by 10,000 B.C., ancient Indian tribes, ancestors of the Hopis, Pimas, Papagos, were living in what is now New Mexico and Arizona. By 7000 B.C., some Indians had reached the extreme southern tip of South America, as shown by remnants of human occupation in two caves of the Fuegian area.

The Navajos, and their relatives, the Apaches, were "late

arrivals," migrating about 1500 A.D. from what is now northwestern Canada to the American Southwest.

In 1540, for the first time Navajos and other Southwest Indians saw bearded men on horseback—with powerful firearms—when Coronado and other Spanish conquistadores reached the Southwest.

Spain, then Mexico, ruled over the Southwest. But the nomadic, autonomous Navajos, who were primarily hunters and raiders, maintained almost complete independence. They learned arts such as weaving; they enormously increased their mobility with horses taken from the Spaniards; and with sheep and goats, brought into the Southwest by the Spaniards, they began to change from warriors to shepherds.

In 1846, the United States took possession of the Southwest territories acquired from Mexico; and from 1846 to 1860 instigated a series of military expeditions against the Navajos to bring "peace and stability."

General James Carleton described Navajos as "wolves that run through the mountains," and sent out an order that "there is to be no council held with the Indians, nor any talks. The men are to be slain whenever and wherever they can be found."

Colonel Kit Carson was given specific instructions to destroy all crops and livestock—to scorch the earth of the Navajos. After most Navajo herds and grains—including the wonderful peach orchards in Canyon de Chelly—were destroyed, the Navajos began the "long walk" to a concentration camp at Fort Sumner in New Mexico, a barren reserve of forty square miles known as the Bosque Redondo, where nearly two thousand died of dysentery and pneumonia, the direct results of starvation.

The forced transplant a tragic failure, the Federal Government in 1868 signed a peace treaty with the Navajos which began: "From this day forward all war between the parties to this agreement shall forever cease." Barboncito signed first, then Armijo, Delgradito, Manuelito, Herrero Grande and seven other Navajo leaders. Manuelito said, "The nights and days were long before it came time for us to go to our homes. . . . When we saw the top of the mountain . . . we felt like talking to the ground, we loved it so, and some of the old men and women cried with joy when they reached their homes."

In the 1880's, the building of the railroads south and east of the Navajo country brought intoxicants, diseases and other disruptive influences of white society to The People. The gradual but steady increase in white population, and the white-owned trading posts, came to mean economic exploitation and a mounting pressure upon the Navajos.

In the early 1920's, the Department of the Interior, through the Indian Commissioner, called for the formation of a Navajo Tribal Council. Navajos then carried out a procedure directed by Anglos, who instructed them to vote "democratically" and allow white men to authorize gas and oil leases on the tribally owned lands. Some Navajos derisively called their councilmen "Oil Chiefs."

We were approaching Albuquerque. I looked out to the Sandia Mountain, noting its rising eastern slope and the sheer, abrupt western face. In a cave high in this western wall, anthropologists discovered the earliest evidence of human life in this area.

At the Albuquerque airport, I walked down a long corridor, found the Econo-Car office and asked Ed Faith, the manager, to rent me a car and point me in the right direction. He unfolds a large map, and his moving finger indicates the line marked U.S. 66, that connects so many of our civilized cities, Chicago to Los Angeles. But my eyes focus on the words LOS ALAMOS, where the atomic bomb was developed. Even in the most peaceful of atmospheres, man devises new weapons of destruction. And throughout our years of "progress," the rate of civilization's rise has corresponded closely with man's ascendant capacity to kill.

In the small rented car on the stretch of desert—the next town, a sign reveals, is seventy miles away—I feel that sense of Aloneness I knew when I first piloted a plane, of being propelled by a motor into space that envelops me.

I continue on to Gallup, New Mexico, called the Indian capital of the world. My father told me of coming here in the 1880's. I drive along a tawdry strip lined by service stations and motels. Faces I see on the streets reveal an interesting mixture of Mexicans, Italians, Slavs, Greeks, and a wide variety of Indians.

I turn off U.S. 66 and cross over into Arizona. In the Navajo capital of Window Rock I drive past a mini-bank, a mini-post office, a gigantic supermarket. I find a motel and check in for the night.

Part II

ON THE RESERVATION

Window Rock, Arizona

I jump into a shower, flip on a TV and there's the "Today" show. I have not yet left my world. Leaving my room I see that the desk clerk, the telephone operator, all those "in authority" are non-Navajos, that is, white people. I walk to the restaurant for the usual ham-and-egg breakfast most white Americans prefer, whether in Keokuk or Kobe, Memphis or Marseilles.

When I pay for my meal, I ask the Anglo at the cash register if he is the manager.

"I *own* it," he boasts. Even though the Navajo tribe owns the structure, the white man feels that he, the tenant, is the real proprietor.

We chat awhile and familiar themes assail my ears. "I know the service is bad, but you can't teach *these people*. In my contract I'm supposed to hire so many, and they are lazy, won't work." I reflect back on the days when I worked as a "black" woman for my *Soul Sister* experiences, and repeatedly heard whites say the same thing about me.

I drive a short distance from the motel to the sandstone formations that give Window Rock its name.

At first glance the oval aperture appears to have been the handiwork of creative stonemasons working with copper and steel tools. But natural artists have fashioned it— wind, sand and water starting back in the Mesozoic era— and like all meticulous craftsmen, working at their own measured pace, without the pressure of deadlines. Navajo medicine men, who traditionally came here to get water used in their religious ceremonies, called the site *Tseghan-*

hodzani—Perforated Rock. But the medicine men left no traces, built no temples, staked no claims in the ways of "organized" societies.

My attempt to discover a "Sense of Place" is futile. It disturbs me that I don't have anything traditional to see or touch, such as some old fortress or the remains of an old Indian temple. But this was never an old Indian settlement; rather it is a new town, "decreed" in 1936 by a white man, John Collier, former Commissioner of Indian Affairs.

Standing here, I recall walking old cobblestoned streets in other capitals, Tegucigalpa in Honduras, Quito in Ecuador, La Paz in Bolivia and the old Inca capital of Cuzco. I could see then that these were originally Indian cities, where even today the people remain predominantly Indian, holding onto much of the Indian culture, modes, rhythms and designs of everyday life. I remember Sacsahuaman fortress, built by early Peruvians using stones weighing thirty tons, and an old Inca temple so perfectly constructed that I couldn't insert a needle between its massive stone blocks. I think of the ruins of old Inca roads that traversed the Andes. And the beautiful woven tapestries that rival the finest ever made anywhere, anytime.

It disturbs me that here in Window Rock I can grasp no handle to the past. I remember my first visit, how I discussed the differences among Indian cultures with my brother Ed. Didn't the Navajos do anything? Build anything? I asked. He explained that their philosophy was to pass through life like birds on the wing, fish in the sea, without leaving a trace on the landscape.

He made it sound very poetic; but I was appalled by a race of people who left *nothing* to show for their time on earth. The Indians in North America must be much younger, culturally speaking, than the Indians to the south, I suggested.

"But they're not," Ed replied, adding: "Artifacts found in the North American continent are as old as anything found in Central and South America."

Well, I blurted out, how come the Indians down south were so much more "advanced"? Why would the same Indians who settled in the Southwest and did *nothing*—comparatively speaking—have brothers and sisters moving on to Mexico, Central and South America, creating civilizations that utterly astounded the Spaniards, and are still sources of wonder and awe to visitors today? Ed listened patiently while I enumerated Aztec, Mayan and Inca achievements: they created strong governments, sophisticated calendars and mathematics, marvelous architecture; they had leaders of remembered distinction.

"Yes, all that's true," he agreed.

And, I asked, what were *our* Indians doing all this time? I had seen nothing here that remotely resembled Cuzco, and I specifically mentioned fortresses and temples.

"Temples—there's your clue," he replied. "The Aztecs, Mayans, Peruvians all had organized religions. In every era, religions have given political institutions the justification, incentive and heart to exist. A strong priest who controls the people can also organize them, set thousands to building roads, pyramids or temples.

"The Navajos never had religious leaders who grasped for power and control over the multitudes. Unlike the settled social orders of other ancient races in Egypt, Peru, Mexico, and most other 'civilized' countries of the world, they had no impulse to erect pyramids, temples, and other conceits of power-driven rulers—or to wage 'holy crusades' and bloody 'religious' wars.

"It is sad," Ed said, "but as man gets more 'civilized' he gets more violent."

Certainly the Incas, whom I had touted as so "civilized,"

had in fact earned a reputation as the New World's most feared conquerors until the arrival of others with more powerful weapons.

"I am convinced that in the early days Navajos went to war merely 'for fun,' for a kind of gamesmanship to test young men," Ed said. "With our cruel wars—and what can have been our excuse for our violence in Vietnam!—one must ask: was not the 'uncivilized' way of the Navajos more peaceful and in this respect more 'civilized' than our own?"

I know that eventually I will "pass" out of my whiteness and turn "Indian," and on that day the Bureau of Indian Affairs—the BIA—will become my Big Brother, or Great White Father. The Indians occupy an alien enclave in our midst, and Washington has a special bureau to "govern" them. No other racial or ethnic group, such as blacks or Chicanos, suffers from this "alien" status.

In my father's day we "governed" Indians with guns. Then we took land "legally" by leases. The BIA was created presumably to "protect" the Indians, but the 4,000 treaties and statutes signed were eventually broken by the protector.

From my motel room, I go to the BIA building, step inside and walk down a long hallway, and have the distinct impression that I'm back home in the nation's capital, in a maze of bureaucracy. I see white "bosses" behind impressive desks and attractive Indian girls, many wearing wigs and mini-dresses, taking dictation and answering telephones.

In one office, I chat with an Anglo, Fred Johnson, who tells me he's been with the BIA for twenty years.

I tell Mr. Johnson I'm interested in knowing just how, legally speaking, the BIA came to "govern" Indians.

"If you read the U.S. Constitution, it says—Congress has the power to regulate . . . Indian tribes. Congress delegated the power to the Department of Interior. And the Department of Interior delegated it to the BIA," he con-

45

tinues. "So the BIA Commissioner has the power to make regulations governing Indians."

He pauses to make sure I'm following, then:

"The Federal courts have held Federal regulations have the power and force of Federal law. Therefore, *the BIA 'governs' Indians.*"

If Washington first described Indian nations as "sovereign," then, I ask, how do we define this tribe today?

"It's a 'quasi-sovereign' body," he replies.

That sounds as improbable a state as quasi-pregnant. I ask Mr. Johnson what it means.

He chuckles and gives me a little wink as if to say we both understand words mean just what we want them to mean. Obviously, he admits, the term confuses the Indians. Then he adds, "But I think it means that whites have never been able to agree that tribes have jurisdiction over *whites* even when a white commits an offense against an Indian on the reservation. If the tribes were 'sovereign' they would have such power."

I ask Mr. Johnson if he thinks the BIA will one day be governed by Indians, and he says, "Yes, we are allowing them to take over."

The implication was clear. Those who "allow" privileges can also take them away.

Leaving the BIA building, I cross over to the Navajo Tribal Council chamber that serves as the congressional unit for the Navajo tribal government, the largest and one of the most sophisticated of Indian bodies. The seventy-four-member Tribal Council represents the reservation's 102 chapters.

The chapter is the smallest geographical subdivision within the Navajo tribal political structure. Chapter meetings, consisting principally of reports made by local public officials and discussion of matters of community interest, are generally attended by from thirty to three hundred local residents. The chapter thus serves as bridge between the "central government" and individual Indians.

A council session is scheduled this morning, and members have begun to drift in. I sit on a wooden pew reserved for visitors. Nearby a Navajo mother, wearing pleated skirt and velvet blouse, with tennis shoes and white socks, holds an infant. Like me, she is intent on absorbing as much of the proceedings as possible. This may be her first time in Window Rock, her first time to see her government at work.

Many of the councilmen are wearing cowboy boots, trousers, shirts, western hats. I study one councilman; he might be almost interchangeable with a Texas rodeo-circuit cowboy I once knew called "Shorty." He wore a white hat and we went to the western picture shows and watched "good" cowboys kill "bad" redskins. Now these Navajos have adopted the dress of their former adversary.

The Indian who has reminded me of "Shorty" surprises me by walking over, extending a hand and introducing himself: "I'm Don Noble, councilman from Steamboat." He is perhaps forty, with bronze skin, abundant black hair and broad shoulders and chest. To be a successful politician one must like to talk—and Noble is no exception.

He gives me a terse briefing on the makeup of the present body:

—The Navajo councilmen are elected by district, and make $7,000 a year. The tribe's chairman is elected at large for a four-year term and makes $18,000. In November, 1970, more than 80 percent of the registered voters went to the polls and elected Peter MacDonald to succeed the incumbent Raymond Nakai.

—The chairman deals with the outside world, especially Washington, but Navajos seldom give individuals complete authority for decision making. It's the Tribal Council, not the chairman, that makes the important decisions.

—The "worthless" land Navajos were permitted to return to in 1868 later proved to have oil and gas and coal and uranium. There's a tribal-owned sawmill, and uranium mines, coal mines; the main income is from oil leases.

—The tribal government has about 200 million dollars in assets and more than 67 million dollars in cash deposits and investments.

At 10:25 A.M., the tribal chairman walks in unobtrusively and quietly takes his seat. Speaking Navajo, he opens the meeting. A veteran of World War II and the first college graduate ever to head the Navajo Nation, Peter MacDonald—in his forties, with dark business suit, horn-rimmed glasses—could "pass" for a college professor or the chairman of any large Anglo corporation.

There's a roll call—sixty-two members are present—and then an Indian delivers the invocation entirely in Navajo except when he calls the name of Jesus Christ. I am the only Anglo in the assembly hall and I am somewhat startled to hear the words *Jesus Christ.*

The councilmen discuss oil, coal and mining rights on the reservation, and a lingering dispute with the Hopis over land they share.

The "unity" of the Navajos was traditionally expressed in a common language. But today no councilman talks five minutes without using an English word to convey his meaning.

From the Tribal Council, I go to the judicial building to visit Chief Justice Virgil L. Kirk. I met him when I visited Navajoland in 1969, and told him then that someday I would return to live on the reservation to research a book.

"Why don't you go sit in court?" he suggests, adding that Judge William Leupp is winding up proceedings on an attempted rape case.

"The defendant has admitted guilt," the chief justice

says, adding, "A guilty Navajo seldom pleads not guilty. It's a basic simplicity and honesty in him."

I suggest that so many Navajos pleading guilty must make it easy for the judge in handing down a verdict.

"We don't think we have an 'easy' job because we do not attempt to act arbitrarily to satisfy 'the law.' Rather we will talk with contending parties until they shake hands, until all agree to the 'justice' of a decision," Justice Kirk says.

"Navajos, believing that only lawless people need many laws, are distrustful of a very complicated legal system. They stress compensation, rather than revenge and retribution. If you are a poor Navajo mother and someone murders your husband, how will it help you if I 'punish' the murderer with a death penalty? No, it would help you more if that man had to chop wood for your family for the next ten years. Or, supply you every year with sheep and blankets."

In a small courtroom I take a seat in the back row. Navajo Judge Leupp looks stern and impressive in his black judicial robe.

The defendant, a sullen, passive-looking youth in his early twenties, admits he drank too much and became aggressive. The assault victim is an overly plump girl of about nineteen, who wears the traditional fluted skirt and calico blouse with a kerchief tied securely around her head. No one seems agitated or even angry.

Judge Leupp is not a lawyer, and neither are any of the young Navajos who speak on behalf of the defendant and prosecutor. They are advocates trained in the law. The Navajos have never had any lawyers, but in 1972 there were a dozen Navajos in law schools.

When Judge Leupp has heard all arguments in the rape case, he sentences the defendant not to prison but "to work for five years" for the family of the girl he has assaulted. And the young man must live in the hogan with the girl and her family.

After the "case dismissed" signal is given, I meet Judge Leupp who tells me his verdict "is not an unusual one. In the past, tribal elders always tried to insure that the injury suffered by a family was compensated for, rather than that their pride was assuaged. Our belief is that if the culprit makes a suitable restitution to his victim no further punishment is necessary. In this rape case, the young man who fathered a child must now work for the child. And after his five years are up, he'll probably want to stay with the family and his child," Judge Leupp says, adding: "We believe there is a limitation to the effectiveness of force, criminal punishment and prison sentences as a solution to problems of law and order."

I walk into the Great Western Bank & Trust that's got a sign outside as big as the building itself; and present a personal check and credentials to a balding, nervous white man, Orson W. Rogers, perfectly typecast from dress to demeanor as a small-town banker.

He is counting out dollar bills to me when an Indian woman wearing six yards of purple pleated skirt and a red velvet overblouse approaches in a flat-heeled stride and puts down her personal check. Rogers gives her a short, emphatic "No."

She walks away, and I long to run after her and explain that I have all sorts of credit cards—American Express, Carte Blanche—and that she does not have these credentials.

"She's done that before!" the banker tells me, unable to contain his frustrations. "She could learn . . ." and his words indicate what we generally think about foreigners and American Indians: why can't they be like you and me?

On my Navajo Nation map, I see the town of Kayenta with the caption, "Most remote Post Office in the United States."

Leaving Window Rock, I drive north, passing through vistas that stretch out to other vistas, into a virtual nothingness, a vastness that is almost celestial in scope. I look out to red-rock canyons, and barren mesas and I reflect on what the councilman, Don Noble, said: the Navajos were given this land because the Anglos deemed it worthless. But now Anglos come in increasing force to take minerals from the soil, to build huge power plants, that in the end will perhaps benefit the big cities but destroy the Navajo. He is *of* the soil—an appendage to this rock-ribbed, rugged land that is not land so much as high mountain ranges and abysmal gorges, all rock and sand. When I catch a glimpse of an Indian in this long-as-time, wide-as-imagination landscape, he appears dwarfed by space, an inconsequential transient—seen one fleeting second, gone the next.

The sacred number *four* permeates Navajo thinking; and Navajoland lies between four sacred mountains: Mount Blanca, San Luis Valley, Colorado; Mount Taylor, north of Laguna, New Mexico; San Francisco Peaks, near Flagstaff, Arizona; and Mount Hesperus, La Plata Mountains, Colorado.

This terrain is part of what geologists call the great Colorado Plateau province of Arizona, New Mexico, Utah and Colorado. The Colorado and San Juan Rivers were boundaries of the Navajo reservation's northwestern territory until they were lost in the rising reservoir behind Glen Canyon dam and ceased to be rivers.

Viewing Navajoland—like viewing the ocean for the first time—is a spiritual experience. I am awed, even shocked by its magnitude. Only the sky is equal to the land. The sky looms larger than half the world, its turquoise dominating the red-orange-brown-yellow lithic world below.

I gaze out, but the vastness responds with glacial aloofness. How can I enter into this vastness, learn to know the place and the people?

In Korea, Malaysia, Turkey, Arabia, I would squeeze myself onto a third-class train or vintage bus, and, careening over mountains and across deserts and into isolated villages, I absorbed some of the local sights, sounds, smells, and so for a moment in time experienced a Sense of Place. I talked with people in words, when this was possible; also I learned their songs, danced their dances; I always ate the local food and drank the local water. And some cautious souls warned: one day you'll die, but—this will happen to us all.

Navajoland will be more difficult to know than the "foreign" lands I have visited. Here I can't mingle and mix with the people, not at once, in any case. I miss the opportunities that I had in Mexico, Malaysia and Peru of boarding buses crowded to the rafters with men, women, children, chickens—sitting up close, seeing the land not just with two eyes but partially through other eyes.

This is the only large portion of the United States that you can't see from the window of a Greyhound bus; and no trains whistle across its vastness. And it is the only large segment of the United States where many of the people still travel to a distant trading post or a windmill by horse-drawn wagons. The Navajos who can afford vehicles generally have pickup trucks. But there are few roads.

Near Coyote Canyon I pick up a hitchhiker, a lonely-looking old man who explains that he is almost blind and can't see left and right, but can recognize the road that lies ahead. Though age has withered his body and taken his sight, I see chuckle lines drawn all over his face. I remain totally silent; on getting in the car he has revealed he knows English, but I do not wish to crowd him. I'm grateful to have the body there beside me. The miles slip behind us, eternity lies all around. Eventually he asks:

"You know where the cluster of trees are?" and he nods his head in the direction to my left. "That's where I was born."

The rock, the cluster of trees, the stream of water . . . all important to this Navajo. Not a designation such as—Have you heard of Lubbock, Texas, that's where I was born. Not a townsite, named to commemorate a man, and man-made, but a site that God made. Place names are most simple, like Tees Toh, "Cottonwood Springs" and Kai Chineldlo, "Willows Line Out Like Braids." I recall others: By the Rocks of Many Waters . . . Green Valleys Coming Together . . . Mouth of the Canyon. Such sites are as well known to the Navajo as our cities to the average American.

Riding on a subway in New York, I passed more people in fifteen minutes than this isolated old Navajo who sits beside me could meet in a dozen lifetimes. I did not feel "related" to any of the thousands upon thousands of civilized men and women I "met" who were rushing to their jobs in the skyscrapers.

Yet I feel a deep affinity with this old man. He has told me where he comes from but I have not told him anything, and he is curious.

"What are you doing out here all by yourself? Where is your family?" he asks me as we roll along like a capsule through space. Before I answer he asks:

"Where is your husband?"

I tell him: I'm looking for a husband.

"Oh! He ran away, did he? Maybe," he volunteers with a chuckle, "he ran off to California? Have you looked over in California?"

He indicates that I should drop him off near a clump of trees, just before we reach the Lukachukai trading post. He expects a relative to pass by and to pick him up at this clump of trees. And I leave him there.

I continue alone—through a desert that is not flat but is broken by chains of mountains. This scenery reminds me of a mirror. I look out—but it turns back on me. The aloneness, the emptiness. Me—lost in space.

One can't subjugate vastness. I want to reduce the landscape to my visual scope, even to my ability *to embrace*, but its "soulless image" awes and overpowers me.

It is after dark when I see a big familiar neon sign, so bizarre in this environment, beckoning me toward—a Holiday Inn!

I park in front of this oasis in the desert, and go in to register. A Navajo policeman walks up with the authority of one who carries a gun. I step aside.

"I'd like a room," he tells the clerk.

A white woman pushes out a registration card but doesn't say anything. "What does a room cost?" the Navajo asks. "Fourteen dollars," the woman replies. "Ohh . . ." and the Navajo repeats the price, "fourteen dollars." And I see him walk away. If he himself, with his wage, is not poor, then others—relatives, in-laws—are. Eighty percent of reservation Indians have a family income below the poverty level.

I pull out my identification card, sign in, get a key—and see that an Arizona State Police car has driven up and two white patrolmen walk up as if they own the place. They do not ask about prices.

"You want your regular rooms?" the clerk asks.

"Yes," they reply, adding, in a jostling vein: "Unless you've let some Indian have it."

I drive the Volks to my motel room, get out my bag, carry it up a flight of stairs. Unlock the door, and inspect my home for the night. I handle the cellophane-wrapped drinking glass, study the sanitized toilet seat, check out the reading lamp by the bed. I finger the writing paper, read over the breakfast menu, note that I may have "room service." In any other town in the United States, I would take these "luxuries" for granted. But not in Navajoland.

When I go to the dining room, I see it is filled with Anglo tourists. A Navajo waitress in a mini-skirt takes my order and I see she wears a curly wig. Is she ashamed of her *straight* Indian hair?—in the way blacks once were ashamed of *curly* hair? She has painted her face with a grotesque theatrical harshness: pancake makeup, false eyelashes.

Traditionally, the Indian woman has never worn makeup of any kind. She has never been to a beauty shop. She has never curled her hair. She has not worn clothes that called attention to her breasts, her legs, her buttocks, as this young woman now does. In the Anglo "feminine" way this Navajo waitress is advertising herself, all of her body one sign: get it if you can.

When I pay my bill I invite the restaurant manager, a man who identifies himself as Dillard Crawley, to have a coffee with me. His family, along with one Harry Goulding, were among the first white traders in his region. He says he finds that "from time to time I must escape the reservation, and I get in my car and drive to Flagstaff. Anyplace you want to go, anyplace where there's a good bar, it's about two hundred miles in any direction." The selling of liquor is illegal on the reservation, but I notice there's an unfinished bar back of the dining room.

I ask: Is he going to open the bar when they legalize liquor on the reservation?

He discusses that possibility, but then adds, "If we open the bar the problem will be: how do you keep *them* out of the place? I wouldn't want to see that lobby filled with drunken Indians."

But, I suggest, if he sells it by the drink the place won't be filled with drunks.

"Oh, you just don't know these drunk Indians!" he replies.

And I recall an evening in the Window Rock restaurant when I sat next to a table of whites, one of them loudly and lewdly drunk, but no one said, Look at that drunk white man, as one might say, Look at that drunk Indian. When a white man gets drunk he's drunk, but a red man becomes *another* drunk Indian.

I study Dillard Crawley—about forty, bright face, clean shirt. I know that since he's lived in this area for many years I might learn from him. I tell him some idle thoughts I've had along the way: how I have easily identified with persons, such as a Korean, and learned to love the place through a person. I explain that I have not felt any telltale signals of "attraction" between me and an Indian man. And that I asked myself: If I want to love a Navajo, why don't I love a child?

"Yes," he replies. "There's Mary Harris, in Page, the daughter of old-time traders. She adopted three little Navajo girls, and raised them. They are just the nicest teen-agers you could meet. I used to think it was hereditary," he adds, meaning that the Navajos were congenitally inferior people. "But now, seeing these girls, I believe it is environmental."

To prove his point he stresses, "You can't even tell they are Navajos."

Mary Harris has given them the greatest of all gifts— she has erased all traces of Navajo from them, made them Good like her, Good like the Anglo.

Morning: Dillard Crawley joins me for coffee. I tell him I'm interested in living with a "typical" Navajo family, in a hogan. Even the name interests me. Hogan sounds Irish.

"It's spelled *qoqán* in Navajo and simply means home,"

Crawley says. "But you've seen them. Probably not up close, or you wouldn't want to live in one."

Didn't Navajos ever build wigwams or tepees? I ask.

"No," Crawley says. "Other Southwestern Indians, including the Hopis, settled in pueblos or cities and have always lived in houses made of rock; but the Navajos became sheepherders instead of farmers, and they built their hogans where their stock could graze. They built what they call their winter or real home and an even more simple summer brush shelter.

"The hogan is a uniquely Navajo development," Crawley continues. "It's a good design and practical; it heats with a minimum amount of fuel, it is cool in summer, and having no windows, it is a retreat from the strong winds. It was a good home for peoples eons ago. But you will be miserable."

When I insist that I've traveled a lot and don't mind a few discomforts, Crawley says, "One of my employees here, Juan Tsosie, can arrange for you to stay with his wife's people in Monument Valley. The name is White Horse. And I'll ask Juan to drive you there; he can use my Land Rover so you won't get stuck in the sand."

He introduces me to Juan Tsosie, a short, stocky Navajo with a broad head set on broad shoulders. He wears cowboy boots, denim pants and jacket. His simple clothes set off his impressive turquoise-and-silver belt buckles, bracelets, rings.

Tsosie, who speaks fluent English, tells me that he will make arrangements for me to visit with his wife's parents, and we agree to leave in two days.

I will leave the Volks here in Kayenta, with my suitcase in it. I decide to travel with only a small handbag. I will wear a Navajo skirt and blouse that I purchased at the Fed-Mart in Window Rock. Navajo women have told me,

"We appreciate your dressing like us." Also, I want to become accustomed to the clothes now, so that I will feel natural wearing them when I "pass" for a Navajo.

One Navajo woman told me, "You will have no problem looking like an Indian. I would not consider that further and no need to do anything—there is such a diversity that there is no 'Indian' look. Of course, a Navajo would know you are not a Navajo, but another Indian would not. Also some tribes permit people to be members with less than one fourth blood which the Navajo requires."

Driving to Monument Valley, Tsosie talks to me about his "sacred" world of the hogan, about his myths that tell how the Holy People built the first hogan of turquoise and white shell, and why the door must always face east, "the direction of all good. And the rising sun and a new day."

He relates how Navajos bless their home, "by putting corn pollen, our symbol of fertility, along the walls, and praying—*hozhoo lelgoo' ot' e*—let this home be a happy home."

Monument Valley lies on the Arizona-Utah border. A sign notes the remoteness of populated centers:

Albuquerque	329
Denver	511
Grand Canyon	156
Los Angeles	666

We ride along a corrugated road, leading to an area billed as the "Eighth Wonder of the World." I see no other vehicle on the road, and when we enter the valley it lies before us and seemingly for us alone. It is free of gawkers and strangely quiet.

I look out to a land that was under the sea some seventy million years ago. About the time the Rocky Mountains were born, this Monument area arose from the ocean, cracked and wrinkled from its long immersion, and then the sand and wind started the process of carving the monuments.

I recall my brother's remark that "God was drunk when

he made the cities but at his creative best when he made Monument Valley."

At the side of a cliff Tsosie points to the Ute Mountains in Colorado, the Henrys in Utah, the Carrizos in New Mexico and the Lukachukais in Arizona. In the clear, dry air at the mile-high altitude, monuments rising 1,000 feet above the plains seem only a stone's throw away, though in fact, they are many miles distant.

The valley, Tsosie reminds me, was the locale for many John Ford westerns including *Stagecoach, Billy the Kid, Kit Carson, My Darling Clementine, She Wore a Yellow Ribbon, How the West Was Won, Fort Apache*—and many others. He has them memorized like a tourist guide.

Tsosie points out a few of the "monuments"—Three Sisters, Big Chief and Totem Pole. I recall having seen Totem Pole, a 500-foot obelisk, larger at the top than at the base, pictured in the *National Geographic* some years ago. Soaring almost as high as the Washington Monument, it was considered impregnable to mountain climbers until four men drove steel pins into rocks and hauled themselves up in what the *Geographic* had called a "perilous assault."

Tsosie points out they were *white* men, and he adds: "The Navajos try to live in harmony with nature, we regard all of the world's creations, animate and inanimate, as *alive*. We call the land Mother Earth. We do not try to overcome nature, to bend nature to man's laws or his will—nor to *assault* her, for any reason."

In Tsosie's words I discern one of the primary differences in Anglo and Indian philosophies.

Western man's phrase "conquest of nature" reflects the illusion that all natural forces can be entirely controlled. It expresses the belief that nature is to be considered primarily as a source of raw materials and energy, that all of the world, in fact, was created for Western man to assault, to conquer.

When Anglos now speak of protecting *our* environment, we assume that man is the sole judge of what should be saved, that he can save what is an essential part of nature and thus control nature itself. Man can control his own actions, but the environment is not and never was our environment. As the Indians know, it belongs not just to us two-legged creatures but to the whole of life.

We drive deep into the recesses of the canyon and at last we come upon "the home," the hogan. Nothing has prepared me for this dismal sight. It has been built of sticks chinked with mud and bark. It has no windows. At a glance, it looks like an upheaval of earth, piled into a barren heap. I unconsciously clutch the seat of the Land Rover. For a moment, I want to return to the known world of Sealy mattresses, telephones, automobiles, the corner drugstore, the assured, easy way.

Tsosie, unaware of my thoughts, reacts to his homecoming like a nine-to-five IBM executive who, returning to his $100,000 suburban home, finds his two-car garage empty. He remarks, quite casually, "I guess everyone is away, but my wife should be returning soon with her parents."

The stories about the hogan had sounded so sweetly innocent. From the outside my impression is that this hogan is only slightly larger than the "play" houses my brothers Harry and Ed used to make with adobe bricks. Once my brothers abandoned one of their mud-brick houses, and I, going there alone, dreamed how one day I might grow up and live there with my playmate Louis, and my dream was one of cleaning, and planting trees and shrubs and flowers to give beauty to our lives.

Looking around this upheaval of dirt called hogan, I see no trees, no yard, no bushes, no flowers, no softness. No, I remind myself, I am in a desert. Only sand. And a house that on first glance seems to have been molded by some giant Ant people, and not by twentieth-century man.

My steps slacken. I feel a moral repugnance, and it weighs on me more heavily than when, researching my book, *Black/White Sex,* I had lived among "the ladies" who sold their sex for pay. But their house was *clean.* They had wooden floors, carpeting and central heat and all of our modern luxuries.

We stand before the wooden door; Tsosie pushes it, and it opens and I step inside, and it is like walking into a dismal, lightless dungeon.

As my eyes grow accustomed to the darkened recesses, I see that simple shelves, to the right of the entrance, have been made from empty orange crates or boxes. A few cracked and oddly matched dishes and old, smoke-stained pots line the shelves. Sheepskins, that serve as beds and covering at night, are stacked on the west side of the hogan.

Clothes are hung on nails or pegs driven into the sides of the hogan walls. Boxes and old, tattered suitcases, evidently with additional clothes and personal belongings, are stacked under the eaves.

I hear in my mind's memory the words of my father: *simplify . . . simplify.* When I had gone into Amazon huts I reflected on his words and then wondered: but how simple can you get? And can one really go backward, to a way of life this simple?

Tsosie is gone. And I am alone. I walk through sand that comes up to my ankles, fills my shoes. I turn occasionally to keep the hogan as my landmark so that I will not get lost. But land that at first glance appears perfectly horizontal undulates, and devours my landmark. The changing angle of the sun gives new light to the rock formations and the red sea of sand. I hold my eyes steadfast on the flat tops of the brilliant turrets that mark the level of the vast plateau. My eyes do not blink, yet colors and vistas have changed.

Stone is the dominant material. Vegetation, when I find it, seems lost in the awesome open spaces. Moment by moment I see the valley and its monuments growing in size, and feel myself diminishing. I recall having this same sensation when I was in a small boat, out of sight of land. I cannot comprehend this greatness, but can only grow small, humble, worshipful before it.

I walk to a flat rock that is built high off the ground like my mother's bed, and I sit, then lie upon it, and ask the sun to bless me: come to me, eternity, tell me what age is like, and dying; but how would you know of these mortal musings? You have no age, or concern for birth, or death. Man, dust to dust returneth, and all other living forms are but transient aspects of your permanent being. You remain always young and whole.

Looking into the valley I sense this permanence, this timelessness, this antiquity in the silence. Gods, it seems, never speak in words when they want to tell you something big.

In the depths of his being, man feels a "love," a reciprocity with nature. And in other lands—and I think especially of my first trip to the lakes of England and to the south of France—I so easily felt a "love" for mountains, lakes, and the gentle, rich yet subdued landscapes that were built to my picture postcard scale.

But here in this region of wind-eroded stone, I and all mankind are so inconspicuous as to seem no more than a trivial accident. I cannot speak of "love" for this creation, I would as soon speak to the thunder or a storm at sea.

I am the only living soul, as far as I can see or hear, an insignificant transient on a stage set billions of years ago. I listen but hear only the silence. The buzz of a fly is amplified. A puff of wind rustles like taffeta past my ear. An hour passes, with no man-inspired distraction until a jet fighter plane streaks across the sky, leaving its trail of vapors to mingle briefly with the clouds.

I walk slowly through the sand back toward the hogan. My steps and life itself move in slow motion. I feel that I am on a long ocean voyage when one surrenders to time.

There's a pickup truck sitting beside the mud house, and it looms, somehow, in my blurred vision, larger than the hogan, and infinitely more appealing as a link to my receding world.

The family is back, I am no longer alone in this world of sand and stone.

I will not walk up and present myself and say how do you do, my name is—and what is your name—and I will not expect them even to speak. No one in the White Horse family will say: Oh, Juan told me you would be here. No one will indicate he or she even sees me. They will reveal themselves to me and I will reveal myself to them by what we do.

My years in South American Indian countries have prepared me for this custom. Seeing a stranger for the first time is an unobtrusive, an insinuating, process. It is as indirect as a quick glance. But you try to avoid peeking at the same time.

Only people with furniture that has to be dusted and beds that must be made, with things, worry about being accepted. People who sleep on dirt floors will move over a couple of feet and there is room for you.

Evening: One by one I come to know the family: Juan Tsosie's wife Rosie, with her reedlike body and finely chiseled features, and her mother Mrs. White Horse and her stepfather George White Horse.

Mrs. White Horse sits cross-legged on the dirt floor and cuts up pieces of mutton and potatoes to make stew. She wears a long, fluted calico skirt and a purple velveteen blouse, the typical Navajo attire that reflects the Spanish influence and also the fashions worn by the wives of American army officers in the late 1860's at Fort Sumner, the concentration camp for Navajos.

Rosie's mother is the stereotype Navajo squaw, almost as round as she's tall, while Rosie is pared-down, slender, with small, delicate features, and her skin is as white as mine.

There is no Navajo look, no single Navajo physical type because of the mixture of Pueblo blood over the years, as well as an infusion of Ute, Walapai and other strains; also the mixing with the Spaniards and later with the Anglos. About twenty Navajo clans are said to have been started by non-Navajos.

When supper is ready, Mrs. White Horse spreads a well-worn, dirty, torn piece of oilcloth on the ground, and we gather around it, each sitting in the position of his choice, cross-legged or, as I prefer, Japanese style, on my heels. I take a portion of fry bread and using it as a spoon ladle out the mutton stew.

All of us, George White Horse and Mrs. White Horse, Rosie and Rosie's three children, eat without talking, as if the meal is such an important event that all of our attention must be devoted to enjoying it.

We drink coffee, made by boiling water over the grounds. This is the one Navajo beverage—other than water, often contaminated, and bootleg whiskey, that is usually consumed away from the hogan. Even the small children are allowed to drink a little of the coffee, and they, too, like the adults, chew determinedly on tough pieces of mutton.

When White Horse strings out a few words in Navajo, his wife answers with a soft "yes" that comes out sounding *ohhhh.* And then the stillness, the quietness. And silence to the urban ear can be eerie, even maddening. If the word "real" can be used at all, it must be with reference to the only world which is real for us. In this unreal world of silence all of the machines have gone dead, all of the internal combustion engines have collapsed. I feel a thousand years back in time from Henry Ford and Walter Cronkite.

Morning: George White Horse and Mrs. White Horse and Juan Tsosie's wife Rosie and the Tsosie children and I shared the floor last night, all of us stretched out with our feet toward the fire, in a circle, like petals on a flower.

I kept wishing I were anyplace else in the world I'd ever been and with any other sleeping arrangement I'd ever known. I lived in Japan a year and came home to brag how I had gone "native" and slept on the floor. It's not the same. The tatami mats that cover Japanese floors are luxurious compared with the hard earth.

Juan Tsosie, who had business in Kayenta, said he would return for me in two days. Now, like a soldier in combat, I mark off the hours. Or I would, except I have no watch, and I see no evidence of any timepiece. Here it is just eternity.

Last night about midnight I heard in the distance the motor of a pickup truck, and listened as it approached the hogan. Everyone else seemed to be sleeping, but I could not imagine why they were unaware of the motor, as it was loudly obtrusive in the otherwise tomblike silence. The motor stopped just outside the hogan and was followed by loud knocking. Since no one else was aroused, I quickly went to the door, feeling assured that it was

Juan Tsosie, and opened the door, but was astonished to see the tall figure of a stranger, who seemed also surprised to see me. He asked in Navajo—where was Tsosie?

White Horse aroused himself, and told the visitor that Tsosie was spending the night in Kayenta. I returned to the skins wishing I were that lucky. And why wasn't he here with his wife and children? For whatever reason, I could sympathize.

The casual scene of my going to a closed, yet unlocked door and simply opening it contrasted sharply with life in the big cities, where worried residents sometimes use three padlocks on their doors. And afterwards when White Horse and his wife had discussed the visitor's call, I discerned from their tone and a few of their words that they knew the man and knew why he wanted to see Tsosie. Since there are only about fifty families in this valley, they all know each other well.

Morning: I scamper out for my toilet though there is nothing outside the hogan in the way of an outhouse. Nothing but space. I miss the luxury of sitting down on a commode! Everything is a matter of habit, I know, but this is what I miss most about life in the hogan. I don't worry about drinking the water and eating the food and sleeping in my clothes doesn't bother me, and even being smelly doesn't bother me. Already I know I have become one of those "smelly Indians." I understand now why the Navajo women wear layers upon layers of skirts, with no underwear, because it's the underwear that gets smelly, not the body so much as the underclothes.

When I wash my hands in the all-purpose tin basin, I use the same driblets of water, no more than a cup in the pan, that all the others have used. When I pour water from one of the steel drums into a basin, I do it gingerly, as if it were liquid gold, which indeed—in this arid desert —it is.

I have never been in any "underdeveloped" country where water is so precious a commodity.

It's an hour trip by pickup truck to the nearest windmill, where water is taken in steel drums and brought back to the hogan. Before Juan Tsosie bought a pickup truck, it was an all-day trip to the windmill by horse-drawn wagon.

Each time I pour out a cup of water I remind myself of the water I waste at a Washington health club. I exercise, then shower; go to sauna, then shower; go for a swim, then shower. I waste more in one day there than the White Horse family uses in a month.

I am helping Rosie herd the sheep back to the corral when Tsosie drives up in Crawley's Land Rover with a group of five tourists.

One of the tourists, a middle-aged woman with camera in hand, asks Tsosie if she can take a picture of the "Indian women"—meaning Rosie and me. Since I, too, am dressed in Navajo attire, the long skirt and overblouse, we look alike to the tourists.

"Oh, sure," Juan tells her and then I see him whispering something in her ear. Is he telling her to give a tip? I feel ridiculous, both as an Anglo and as an "Indian." Why must the tourist make "us" different?

White Horse is inside the hogan, lounging on the sheepskins, and Tsosie persuades him to come out. Tsosie lines the three of us in a row—for the type picture my grandmother always snapped—and the tourist captures her photo of "real, live Indians" and then hands White Horse a dollar bill.

Tsosie then drives off with the tourists, to show them the remainder of Monument Valley and return them to the Holiday Inn in Kayenta.

George White Horse, whose big chest blends into a belly so that you can't tell where one begins and the other leaves off, wakes—we are all on the sheepskins, in the hogan—and asks, "What day is this? Is this Wednesday?"

One loses track of days, and Wednesday is not really different from Monday.

After our breakfast of fry bread, Rosie saddles a black horse and rides off to herd the sheep. George and I stand around outside the hogan, then walk to the corral, sit on a log. He allows me to follow him around as a dog or a child might do. He's in cowboy boots, plaid shirt, blue jeans. We sit, not talking. And I have the impression that this world of Monument Valley is not real. That the entire "scene" of the hogan and the people and the three children playing in the sand pit that stretches out to eternity has been staged for my benefit. But, in and out of the theater, how does one truly determine what is real and unreal?

Suddenly, White Horse begins talking of a past, and he recalls it unevenly: "I was in the service and I had a white woman. It was in England, World War Two. Many bombs . . . She was an English girl, and she was in the service, too. We'd drink that English black beer, Stout." He pauses so long I fear he's finished the story. "And she liked me. She'd call me, and we got us a room, and then she got with a child. I have a child," and he repeats this three times, glancing occasionally but perhaps not seeing the three Navajo children who are romping about in the sand.

"But we were separated and I never saw her again. Yes, I fought for this country," and he corrects himself: "I fought for *my* country." And there's a hint of irony in his tone, but also a note of pride. Many Navajos only began to see the outside world and to understand something of the culture and the ways of the white man during World War II.

George is a "road chief"; he arranges Navajo religious meetings centered around the use of the hallucinogenic drug peyote.

He shows me separate strings of peyote buttons, each about the size of an overcoat button. "These are hers—" meaning his wife's—and "these are mine," he tells me.

George goes to the Texas border to buy quantities of the "medicine," a term he prefers to peyote. Buttons are taken from small, low-growing hairy cactus.

He tells me about a ceremony for an elderly woman who lives in Monument Valley and suffers from an illness of "the spirit." In this ceremony, the peyote was ground up and everyone drank it, but he also says, "You can take the 'medicine' in any form, whole, green, dried or soaked or ground or boiled." I was curious about its effects.

How does it make him feel? I ask.

"I feel young, I have energy, I can do anything I want. The old ailment I got in the service stops hurting."

I ask: does the peyote "medicine" cure in the same way as herbs?

"No, no," he says. "It is the power that is in the medicine, not the medicine itself. The Holy Spirit is there. He makes you aware. If you are an artificial man the spirit in the Holy Medicine will not come to you." And while he does not specify, George seems to equate being natural with being Navajo, to feel that peyote helps one adhere to the old Navajo life and avoid being destroyed, spiritually, by the artificial white way.

* * *

The next day, Tsosie returns in the Land Rover to take me back to Kayenta. I have my few possessions, a handbag and sweater, in hand. Traditionally the Navajo does not say good-byes. One must leave so he leaves, and superfluous words such as thanks for everything are simply not spoken. I nod to the mother of Rosie and to the others, walk out behind Juan Tsosie and climb up in the Land Rover, and then we leave the hogan in the distance. It is so quickly lost from view, swallowed up so easily by the undulating land that still looks deceptively flat.

As we join the main road leading out of the valley, Juan tells me he plans to go by a trading post before we return to Kayenta. I know Navajos use the trading post as a central clearing house. It serves as the U.S. post office, and a place where Navajos, who do not have telephones or mail deliveries to their hogans, leave messages for one another.

Since Charles Crary, an Anglo, came to Navajoland in 1871 and opened the first trading post, all of the stores selling general merchandise to Indians have been owned and operated by whites. I had asked Chief Justice Kirk: why haven't Indians run the trading posts? He had surprised me by saying, "We don't have Indians who are qualified." *You* are qualified—you, being qualified to be the chief justice, could surely run a trading post, I had insisted. And then he had told me a reason closer to the truth: "Navajos have never been all that interested in money."

Before coming to the reservation, I read figures in Washington showing Navajos must pay almost 30 percent more for the goods they buy on the reservation than is charged the average American consumer. Tsosie now tells me: "Without exception, prices are higher at the trading posts than elsewhere. Coffee, sugar, flour are always marked up. And remember, there's no store across the street. There's no place else for the average Navajo to trade.

"When I was growing up, the trader was the first white man I ever saw," Juan continues. "I was ten before I went to school. And my parents did not know how to read and write. When I'd go with my father or mother to the trading post, I would stand and watch the trader scratch down mysterious figures. My mother or my father did not know what they meant, I didn't know.

"My mother wove rugs, and there was only one place where she could take them, to the trader. He'd scratch down a figure and that was our 'credit' except that we always owed the trader and we never knew why.

"Then my father died, and we got welfare checks. But they came to the trading post—the trader was also the postman—and the trader held the check in his hand while my mother put her fingerprint on it, endorsing it over to him.

"And whenever we had to have cash, my mother would take a turquoise bracelet or necklace or belt—maybe worth three hundred dollars, and the trader might give her fifty dollars and put it in pawn. Once Mrs. White Horse pawned Rosie's bracelet. And when we went to get it the trader said, 'You took Rosie's bracelet out the last time you were here.' But Rosie's mother had never taken it out of pawn. He probably sold it.

"When I was growing up there was nothing, really, we could do," Tsosie says, adding, "but now we have started forming credit unions. By having co-op stores that offer some prices that are lower than the traders', the people will be able to see where they can get most for their money."

We stop at the Oljato (Moonlight) trading post where one expects Marshal Dillon to ride up any moment and hitch his horse.

As we park the Land Rover in front of the old frame building, I see a wrinkled, wise-looking old Indian ride up on his paint horse and tie the reins to a hitching post. He ambles into the building after us. He wears his hair in a chignon, a vertical knot in the back, just as his father and his mother always wore their hair. This is the style for all Navajos, men and women, who keep the traditional way. I study this old man, as I watch my would-be mentor count out coins and hand them to the hard-faced white woman who in turn presents him with a diet cola.

I watch him turn the bottled drink to his lips, and note the look of satisfaction that comes over his face. Why does this tall, pencil-slim Indian want a *diet* cola? I see him, whom I have perceived as having wisdom beyond the grave, gaze longingly toward the tawdry items in the glassed-in showcase. How readily Indians in Honduras, Guatemala, Mexico, Bolivia, Ecuador, Peru—indeed, peoples of the world—become attracted not to the best from the United States but to the crass: blaring jukeboxes, garish neons, gossamer movies, chewing gum and bottled sugary and diet drinks.

Juan Tsosie tells me the trading post has a "museum," consisting of the priceless items that have been pawned by the Indians, and when we ask the white woman behind the cash register if we may see it, she nods toward a tall Navajo woman employee to get the key. This young woman, in her late twenties, who has made up her face as though a camera awaits her next move, unlocks a door to a back room.

My eyes fall upon a large selection of handwoven blankets and rugs, some stacked in piles and others displayed around the wall. "It's the Navajo women who are the weavers," Tsosie tells me. The imagery is strong, bold and decidedly contrary to what's considered the feminine esthetic. Styles range from quiet, plain-stripe patterns of the early 1800's to the eye-dazzlers of the late 1890's, with aggressive designs and colors reminiscent of Op. The rugs are considered priceless rarities in museums.

We inspect handwoven baskets used in religious ceremonies, and countless turquoise-and-silver necklaces, rings, belts, bracelets.

When we leave, to continue on to Kayenta, I reflect: how sad that the Navajos allow their priceless jewelry to slip into the white traders' hands. Why would they not fight to get them back? I look at Tsosie and see that he is not a "militant" man.

I tell Tsosie: if this "museum" were in a black populated area and all of its objects had been taken from the blacks, the militants among them might come one night and reclaim all, saying: you didn't pay us anything for it, and besides, it's rightfully ours. You've cheated us too long. You've got too many back dues.

Juan does not respond with any words. He looks passive, seemingly subdued beyond any individual act of rebellion.

I am back in the Navajo Nation Tribal Council chamber in Window Rock. Navajo councilmen listen intensely as Council Chairman MacDonald accepts the United States' offer to let the Navajo people run their own reservation. He outlines a plan that would, within two years, give the tribe total control of the 110-million-dollar-a-year Bureau of Indian Affairs operation.

MacDonald says: "Although we welcome the offer and certainly will take advantage of it, it will be some time before we can come to terms on things that the BIA at present is not willing to give up."

The bureau wants to retain all civil service employees, thereby curtailing the hiring and firing capacity of the tribe.

Also, the amount of money involved in the takeover is a factor. "We believe," MacDonald explains, "that just taking over the programs at the area level is not sufficient because there are those operating and administrative costs that go all the way into the Interior Secretary's office."

In discussing the BIA proposal, MacDonald also says he is thinking of a new capital city for the Navajo Nation, one built with "Navajo architecture and ideals."

Although the plan for "giving" the BIA to the Indians sounds impressive, the hard core of the BIA remains Anglo, and big changes aren't likely until the Navajos replace the Anglos.

I have been attending classes being offered in the Navajo language at Fort Defiance.

I discovered that Navajo is a highly complex language; it is full of movement, of verbs with subtly shaded meanings whose action may be modified by a wide variety of prefixes.

When I first heard Navajo spoken, it reminded me of the singsong Cantonese I'd heard in Hong Kong. Like Chinese, Navajo is a "tone language," and the meaning of the words is distinguished by the pitch of the voice, whether it be raised or lowered.

My brother Ed, who had studied Navajo, said he had much trouble with the inflections. "When I was trying to learn Navajo," Ed once told me, "Judge Kirk tried to help me pronounce *Shah ha twee* meaning 'Your honor'—but when I used it in front of others, he would say, 'Your Texas accent makes it come out *My husband!*'"

I first met Judge Kirk and his wife at their home in Ship-rock when I came to the reservation on my cursory visit in 1969. My brother Ed drove me there, and we inspected the marvelous Navajo rugs that the judge's aunt had woven and given him. He told me then that she had been selected to exhibit her Navajo blankets and rugs at the 1939 San Francisco World's Fair.

My brother urged, "Get the judge to take you out to Aunt Zonie's hogan. It's out in the piney woods. You will think you are at the end of the world! It's beautiful. And she lives there all alone."

But I knew, from having read a Navajo autobiography, *Son of Old Man Hat,* that Navajos never "live" in just one place for very long. They abandon a hogan whenever there's a death in any one of them—no one wanting to live where dead spirits might reside. And traditionally they moved from winter to summer hogans, living where they could find grazing lands for their sheep.

Judge Kirk told me Aunt Zonie is now visiting with a daughter in a community called Navajo, southwest of Window Rock.

I want to meet Aunt Zonie, and live with her awhile—in her piney woods hogan. I ask Judge Kirk if he will drive me to the daughter's home. He agrees, and he calls for me at the motel. We drive endless miles in the gathering darkness, neither of us saying much. I appreciate the subtle communion of such silences, which often dissolve the sense of strangeness in a way that words never can.

Eventually I ask if Aunt Zonie is his mother's or his

father's sister, and he says neither, that she is a relative by clan.

As an Anglo I am confused when Navajos talk about their mothers, sisters, brothers. They seem to have an unlimited supply of these relatives who are not in fact biologically related. The Navajo social structure is built upon this elaborate clan relationship, in which the mother, father, sister, brother identifications have the reality of the Anglo's "blood kin" and even the Navajos have difficulty explaining the precise nature of the kinships they honor with the fidelity we reserve for members of our immediate family.

How many "sisters," "fathers," "aunts" might he have? I ask the judge.

"Oh, I've never counted them. All members of our clan are 'sisters' 'brothers' 'fathers' . . ."

But how does he tell a clan sister from a clan mother?

"That would depend upon the age. Zonie Lee is my 'aunt' because she's the age of my mother, who died when I was a child. Aunt Zonie raised me. Sometimes I also call her 'mother,'" the judge tells me.

"In the past, a leader of men assumed responsibility for the other members of his clan, and he tried to protect them against murder, theft and debts. Without the 'rule' of church, school or state, the Navajo clan served as an important agency of social control.

"How any one individual is related to you is not so important. You are a member of a Navajo family and the way of life for the Navajos has always been a family way. The basis of the system was and continues to be *the family*," he goes on. "To live, just to survive in this barren land the individual has had to have the economic cooperation of others, and the others were not just those in your own hogan but those who were in your 'outfit'—a wide circle of kin—and those in your clan.

"If a man doesn't do right, the clan gets down on him. But old patterns are changing. Today many Navajos no longer are dependent on the economic support and good will of their relatives. The main reason today why the clan is so important is that it limits marriage choices: you may never marry within your mother's or your father's clan. By outlawing sexual rivalry the clan had greater solidarity. There aren't too many violations of this rule—even today. Although it is changing. And some of the young people today don't even know their own clan."

We drive south and turn off the main road at Navajo. The judge pulls up to a small frame house, the modern evolution of the hogan, and we go inside to a combination bedroom-living room.

I have mentally prepared myself for a purely Indian experience, a walkthrough to a different world and culture, backward in time. I want to be one among them, but upon entering the room—where several Navajo men, women and children are sitting, standing or moving about—the first voice I hear is that of comedian Flip Wilson, emanating from a color TV set. Even more grotesque under the circumstances, he is doing his famous impersonation of Geraldine. It is almost too much for me to absorb. I suddenly realize that the Indians are not very attentive to the TV itself, and that the comedian's voice is more a background noise—and that noise, more than drugs, has become our most rampant, mind-blowing "addiction."

The chief justice assumes center stage—standing, without removing his impressive overcoat and felt hat—but no introductions are made in the Anglo fashion. When there is a stranger in their midst the Navajos have a way of averting their eyes that Anglos find most unsettling. The Western mind views this behavior as indifference or timidity, while the Navajos undoubtedly view our direct approach as rudeness.

We remain quiet, waiting for a time to begin, or perhaps

just for time to run its course. This gives everyone a chance to form his first impressions. I see a woman sitting on the side of a bed with two children and denim-clad Indians, one of whom may be Aunt Zonie's adopted grandson who works at the sawmill.

My eyes expectantly search out and focus on a woman who is in her seventies, weather-beaten and dominant, with gray hair pulled back in a double bun. She wears a long red-white pleated skirt, with several petticoats underneath and a red velveteen overblouse. I know without being told that this is Aunt Zonie. A recognition is exchanged in our glances. It is the only introduction we will have, wordless but complete.

She is shy, but I detect more. Her dark eyes seem also to say—I am woman, but not afraid, I know my worth.

The denim-clad workmen, the mother of the children, the rest of us remain quiet, almost as if we might be friezes. I stand, walk around the room, inquire about a photograph on a wall. It is Aunt Zonie, with one of her award-winning Navajo rugs, taken at the San Francisco fair. She is wearing a long velvet dress, an expensive squash necklace of silver and heavy turquoise stones, as well as a silver, turquoise-studded concha belt, rings and bracelets. The typical Navajo woman never banked her money, she put it in turquoise jewelry.

Eventually, words begin to flow, and Judge Kirk explains to Aunt Zonie what she already seems to know: that I'd like to go with her to her hogan, and she nods her head, obviously pleased with the idea. She reminds me of my mother: say *go,* and she doesn't take five minutes to pack.

This is Monday and it's agreed I'll come back in two days, and we'll go to her hogan.

* * *

Aunt Zonie is ready, her face bright with excitement. She wears her fluted checkered cotton skirt, the red velveteen overblouse. And she holds a traincase, the kind Anglo women fill with creams, rouges, lipsticks, eye shadows. But I know Aunt Zonie never touches cosmetics. Before leaving, she opens the case to check its contents and I see it holds her medicines—prescribed by white doctors.

Zonie's clan granddaughter comes into the room to bid us good-bye, and she leans on her broom. It must seem a thankless chore continually to sweep sand out of the poorly constructed frame house, and she impresses me as a Navajo afflicted by Western man's malaise. Does the idea of "going" appeal to her more than the idea of "staying"? Surely it isn't that she wants to leave her house with its electricity and television for Zonie's hogan with its nothingness.

When Aunt Zonie and I get to the car, she inspects the bags of groceries I've bought at the food market in Window Rock, and reminds me, "Well, my dear, we don't have any meat." She speaks so softly I must get an ear almost next to her mouth to understand.

We drive the thirty miles back to Window Rock and at the big grocery store—the only good place to buy food on the reservation—Aunt Zonie and I go to the meat counter. She gazes with deep concentration. Finally she takes a few steps and again becomes entranced, turning all of her mental faculties to the selection of some mutton. My plan is to get in and get out, as quickly as possible, but apparently her plan is to take as much time as possible.

"No, my dear, I don't like the looks of this mutton," she tells me at last. "The trading post at Fort Defiance will have better mutton." We drive the nine miles to the trading post, and Aunt Zonie enters with as much assurance as she would enter her own home. The owner is a white man whose family has been here for generations, and he greets her in Navajo. The trading post is small, cluttered, with only a small selection of merchandise, all of it overpriced. But the customers are all like Aunt Zonie, wearing long, fluted skirts and double buns. They have, I imagine, come here all of their lives, and pawned their turquoise-and-silver jewelry when they needed quick cash.

No doubt over the years the trader has been "good" to his Indians, but as a former general counsel for the Navajo Tribe, Norman Littell, once pointed out, "only a width of a hair separates paternalism from dictatorship."

In this trading post, Aunt Zonie takes even a greater amount of time. I try to remember that when she was growing up a trip to the trading post was the big event of the month. She got her mail, if any, at the trading post. She got all of her messages there. It was the only "headquarters" that Navajos ever had.

She exchanges gossip with old Navajo women, and half-heartedly selects some very stale fruit. Eventually she goes to the meat counter. She talks, in Navajo, with the butcher, who assures her that he has fresh mutton. And there's the carcass of an old sheep (it's lamb that comes from young sheep) to prove it. I see him take a large butcher's saw and cut out a portion the size of a bass fiddle.

Aunt Zonie nods her approval and I pay nine dollars for our purchase.

Nine dollars! That seems a lot of money for mutton, more so because I have no craving for it. But when Aunt Zonie said, "My dear, we don't have any meat," she meant mutton. Ever since they got their first sheep from the Spaniards, Navajos have made sheep a way of life. And Aunt Zonie seems no exception: when a Navajo speaks about a meal with meat, he means meat from a goat or a sheep.

From Fort Defiance we travel over a winding dirt road,

leaving land that seems bare as bleached bones, with scant grass and no bushes, and climb into an area of creosote, sagebrush, greasewood. As we drive higher into the hills I notice dwarf cedars, scrub oak, piñon, junipers. There is no traffic. No other people anywhere. The world seems pristine, made only for us. On a hill and to our right there's a vast plateau so smooth it invites you to discard your worldly cares, to stop and celebrate its beauty, perhaps to scamper, jump or simply to run as an expression of sheer exuberant release.

I stop the motor. We sit silently. Then I ask Aunt Zonie to tell me about her childhood. She tells me how she herded sheep, walked miles to the nearest well, ground corn, gathered wild greens and piñon nuts. Both of us still look out at the high plains, and such beauty seems to remind us we are here to enjoy, to celebrate our span on earth.

What, I ask Aunt Zonie, was her happiest time?

"When I was young, riding my horse. . . ." and I see her as an image of motion, her body blending with the body of the flying horse, and both wild, not earthbound but liberated in spirit, fleeting like the essence of life, as ethereal as the air or sky.

I add another illusion. She, young, beautiful, happy, riding her mare like the wind—had she *fallen in love?*

No, she tells me, the Navajos do not have the romantic illusions of a young person falling in love at sight and then marrying of his own will. Individuals must comply with family and clan wishes, and work for the welfare of all.

The Navajo way may seem "different" but it's only different from *our* way. In other countries—Japan, Turkey, Peru, Arabia—marriage is more an arrangement between two families than a contract between two individuals.

In the case of Navajo women, "your uncle arranges your marriage," Aunt Zonie says. And to denote that it is an uncle of biological not just clan kinship she calls him her "really" uncle.

"When I was a child, my 'really' mother died and they sent me to another family but they didn't treat me well, and so I ran away to the boarding school at Fort Defiance, and later I went to Albuquerque Indian School. When I was twenty my 'really' uncle said I must get married. I wanted to finish school, I didn't want to get married.

" 'No,' he said, 'you must marry this man because he is a good man and I want you to marry him.'

"My uncle killed two sheep, and many relatives came, and my husband's mother came from Ganado; she was dressed in a beautiful long velvet dress, with much silver-and-turquoise jewelry loaned her by her relatives.

"We went into my uncle's hogan, and he talked to us, about who each one of us was, about our past and our families, and how we must be true, be good to one another. And he fed us the holy corn mush from his fingers, placing it on our tongues.

"My uncle had prepared a special hogan for us, and we stayed there two days. I had no problems. I knew how to cook, I had my own grinding stone for corn. . . ."

Her words echo in my mind, she had no problems, she knew how to cook. How simple her life had been. And when she talks about her husband—"a good man" she tells me and again, "a wonderful man"—it is almost as if I can come to know him, even now, although he has been dead these many years.

"He taught me many things, how to rope cattle and sheep." She has tears in her eyes, and I have no way of knowing whether she is crying because she had struggled to join her life with another life, only to have it wrenched away from her, or whether Aunt Zonie cries as so many of us cry: without knowing why.

All that we know about ourselves and can never say

makes Aunt Zonie and me sad, and there is this sadness in us all. We have tongues but we cannot speak. And when we in the cities talk, then we cover up our sadness.

We have been over rocks, through sand and now we skid over patches of wet pasture. We are at an elevation of 7,000 feet, and I feel I'm on a slalom course as I twist and turn the Volks. I listen for Aunt Zonie's almost inaudible directions of left and right; eventually we make a turn, and there, set almost on the edge of eternity, sits her hogan.

It is a round house, built of logs, with mud plaster roof. It has three small shuttered windows.

Typically, there has been no attempt to decorate the outside of the hogan. In Mexico the natives always have some decoration or flowers out front, but the Navajo way is to consider all of outdoors a "home"—to live outdoors more than indoors.

To live an outdoors type of life struggling against the elements, a woman especially needs a man. The roles become so clearly defined. And the need—one for the other—so apparent. Even when the woman is strong in spirit like Aunt Zonie.

Since her husband died, Aunt Zonie's children and other relatives sometimes tease her about getting another husband, but, she says, she never wanted another man.

" 'You're not too old,' they say and they tell me a man would be good, he could chop the wood, haul the water, but I say, 'No, I had a good man. And I can hire someone to chop the wood and haul the water.' "

We get out and walk to the door. Aunt Zonie fumbles to find the key to the wooden door with its outside lock. In the old days, she and her husband kept only a blanket, one that she had woven, over the door.

We enter a home that has not changed basically in concept or design for hundreds of years; it is a shelter designed for people. But once inside we see it is filled with *things*. Among them, almost overpowering us in their monstrous size in this small setting, are two old, worthless and very dirty mattresses. The mattresses, stood on end, lean against the iron stove that's always in the center of the hogan. One of the mattresses, I note, is king-sized!

Aunt Zonie looks ill at the sight of the old mattresses, and explains that a "thoughtless niece" must have come to the hogan, in her absence, and left the mattresses, as well as other possessions she no longer wanted.

"She could have at least left them in the barn!" Zonie says. Looking about, I see that Zonie is neat and orderly. To the right of the entrance is a simple old-fashioned cupboard for such staples as flour, salt, pepper. The cupboard also contains a few pots and pans, knives and forks, as well as a few dishes.

Before coping with the surplus mattresses, Zonie and I first set about the essentials, making a "home" in an isolated hogan without water, heat, electricity. Our meat and butter and eggs and milk need refrigeration. Where should they go? Aunt Zonie directs me outside to the "ice box." Climbing a ladder to the branches of a pine tree, I stash our perishables in a high-altitude box, made like a chicken coop with meshed wiring to keep out predatory animals.

"Well, my dear," Aunt Zonie says on my return, "we forgot the kerosene." That means we will be without any lights.

I start out to gather wood for the stove.

"First we must go for water," she tells me.

After a search we locate a steel barrel in a barn back of the hogan. Usually Navajos carry barrels of water to and from a windmill in wagons or pickup trucks. After much struggling, we get the barrel in the front seat of the Volks and Zonie climbs in back. We drive twenty miles to the windmill, and fill the barrel with water. None of it is easy; but had we gone by horse-drawn wagon, it would have taken an entire day.

Returning to the hogan, we gather wood and make a fire in the iron stove that serves for heating and cooking. Then we turn our attention to the mattresses that are consuming all of the "living" space in the one-room home. I don't think we can budge the monstrosities. My thoughts turn to getting a man. But where? The nearest neighbor probably is fifty miles out in the piney woods. We go back to the barn, find a wheelbarrow, push it to the hogan and shove the smaller mattress on top. With Aunt Zonie holding the mattress in place, I push the wheelbarrow back to the barn. When we tackle the king-sized mattress, we resemble two ants hauling off a log. We push and shove the behemoth onto the wheelbarrow, but the weight is too much and the wheel rolls off.

"My dear, we'll have to get it on top of the car," Aunt Zonie decides, and because she is determined, we get the mattress there. She holds it over the hood while I reverse the Volks and back it to the barn.

Exhausted by our chores, we eventually get to bed. Aunt Zonie has two small army-type cots, with blankets, and she falls asleep.

The isolation, the silence prevents my sleeping. I am not attuned to this world without humming machines, our background lullabies, as it were, of churning dishwashers, stereos and motors from heaters and coolers, airplanes, buses, automobiles.

I try to imagine living permanently in such isolation, man's natural state, when you consider his 1,000,000 years of history. Since I am unable to sleep, I get out of the cot —I am still in my clothes—and slip on my shoes and reach for my coat. And walking from the dismal darkness of the hut I am almost blinded by the brilliance of the universe.

The landscape, the pines, the sky are etched pure and unspoiled by human intrusions. I recall my life in Washington. Before I left for the reservation, a friend had invited me to a new restaurant. We drove across Memorial Bridge into Virginia, and climbed one of adjoining low hills. We parked, entered a tall building and rode in an elevator with glass walls, reminding me of the cable car that ascends the Hong Kong peak, with its majestic panorama of lights below. I had never seen Washington look more spectacular. The air was clear enough to see in the distance the Lincoln Memorial, the Washington Monument, the Capitol, Kennedy Center. All during the evening, as we lingered over our meal, I kept turning to look *out* to the necklace of lights that man had strung across the sky. I thought of the cavalcade of railroad cars bearing oil and coal, the smoke and sulphur oxides, required to sustain the man-made galaxy.

But what I feel now, in this night, outside Zonie's hogan, is a looking up to the heavens and a looking *out* that is also a looking *in*.

I feel a Presence whose works are more wondrous than man-made monuments the architects in Paris, Athens, Rome could conceive, and more enduring. In the world of science and technology, the moon had become a pocked image on television screens, cold and impersonal, illuminating nothing within, offering neither inspirations nor dreams. The natural world had been compressed into a computer, and something of my soul had been compressed with it.

Morning: I sit outside the hogan, while Zonie, who has been kept awake much of the night by severe coughing, sleeps through the dawn hours. I peek inside one of the hogan windows. She is lying on her single frame bed, in her red-white checkered fluted skirt and red overblouse, rumpled up like a depleted accordion.

Sitting here, outside the hogan, I imagine that I am Zonie, a young woman with a young husband. Two who have everything "in common," sharing the conviction that beauty and happiness are synonymous, qualities to be found in the plants, water, desert floor, mountains.

Reflecting on their "walk through time," I realize that nothing I have ever known could compensate for what I have not known: the struggle just to live. The struggle to get water, to make dough for bread, to chop wood for the fire. To survive.

As Zonie sleeps on, I am reminded of Socrates seeing a parade of rich Athenians displaying their jewelry: Oh, he observed, there are so many things I do not want.

I look around Aunt Zonie's grounds and see what only the "thoughtless niece" could have discarded: a chewing gum wrapper, a Styrofoam cup, a pop bottle, a child's toy.

Will the beautiful life that I imagine Aunt Zonie to have lived be forever *in the past?* Did Zonie and her people not pollute the land because they never really had anything to pollute it with?

Zonie has rested. Didn't she want to stay in bed? I ask. "No, it is not good to sleep too much," she says.

We walk to a nearby lake. Along the way, Zonie stoops and tells me: "My dear, look at this plant." She identifies the name of the plant in Navajo and asks, What is the name in English? With her, in her world, I am so uneducated. I must tell her that I have never seen the plant, or having seen it, did not truly observe and come to know it.

When Aunt Zonie recognizes a plant, she talks with it, treats it very gently, as she would a person who she knows is sensitive, tuned in on the nuances of words and gestures.

I recall once when my mother came to visit me. I was in the bedroom when I heard her speaking solicitously. "Oh, *you* must be very thirsty." I walked into the living room and realized that she was talking with the plants, and not just pouring water on them, but very tenderly giving them a drink. In her own Texas home, she plays music on the radio that she says her plants enjoy. And for her, they flourish.

In my life, I have come to live almost entirely alone, among artificial plants. But Aunt Zonie has lived her life out-of-doors, with all that is natural, life itself—stones, worms, plants, animals. I thought I knew the world, having been *places*. Zonie knows a world I do not know—her knowledge of the plant and animal kingdoms seems inexhaustible. She tells me that Navajos have recorded five hundred plants, and they have classified sixty as edible and thirty as having narcotic, stimulant or medicinal properties.

In the "drugstores," of their fields, Indians found such essentials as diapers, pain-killers, shampoo, even birth control pills. The women relied on stoneseed, a common weed, for an oral contraceptive.

"If you get a fever or get a headache, Indians treat it with the preserved bark of willow steeped in boiling water," Zonie says.

"We name plants on their sex, their medicinal properties and their feel, or appearance.

"In our religious chants, each plant and animal corresponds with a natural element," she continues. "A crane is associated with sky; a red songbird, the sun; an eagle, the mountain; a hawk, rock; bluebird, tree; hummingbird, plant; cornbeetle, earth; and heron, water.

"The Indian people know about the animals," Zonie tells me, "because we have lived here thousands of years, and have passed the knowledge from one generation to another. In our mythology, men long ago married the animals and acquired this knowledge from their animal wives."

Was this myth true? I ask Aunt Zonie.

"What myth, my daughter?"

That your ancestors married the animals?

"Yes," she replies after a moment. "My grandmother married a horse."

And I want to ask her, did you mean it, was that true, but she is acting older and more deaf than the rocks in these hills; with her I am a child of seven when I went to grandmother's house and played along the creek, and all the world consisted of such mysteries as how caterpillars turned to butterflies, how tadpoles came with rain and how all plants, even as Aunt Zonie reminds me now, have different faces, even different personalities, some prickly, others soft, smooth, or sticky.

"This plant has a good smell," she says and I sniff and do not sense any odor. It is like attempting to recognize the bouquet of a subtle beaujolais when one has never tasted wine.

We come to a cluster of wild flowers. I want to stop, break them, keep them.

"No, my dear," Aunt Zonie chides me, reminding me that "Indians never pick flowers, not for pleasure. They have sacred uses known only to the wise people."

Sacred uses. Momentarily I feel that I must tiptoe, that I am in the presence of a spirit. And then, I come back to my own ego, the ego of Western man: only he is sacred, holy. Plants, flowers, animals, all else is put here for his use.

I see Aunt Zonie lift an herb, used among the Navajos to cure toothache, earaches and rheumatism, as gently as if it were a living *soul*.

"When the Medicine Man gathers roots or leaves or bárk for medicines, he places a small offering at the site, for he believes that the soul of the plant must cooperate, that without the soul the mere 'body' of the plant can work no cures."

What might his offering be?

"He might leave some money, or some tobacco, and when he takes the root he says a prayer: 'I have taken what they have given, and I am leaving this for you. I want to lead a long life and to have no harm strike me or my family.' "

I see a tree with piñon nuts. "Every three or four years there's a crop of these nuts," Zonie tells me.

Oh, that would be a good business! I respond. I recall what I have paid for the nuts in Washington, D.C. Why, I ask, hasn't an Indian taken over the piñon market?

Zonie keeps walking, and again her mind returns to the beginning, the long ago, and how it was with her, her husband: "We took from the earth only what we needed. We took the piñons when we needed them.

"My husband had a bow and arrow, and he killed game if we needed it. Sometimes a deer, a rabbit, and we gathered wild greens and the piñon nuts, but only when we needed them."

Aunt Zonie leaves me, returns to the hogan; and I sit by the lake, then stroll among the pines. I listen to a distant woodpecker. And to the wind in the pines.

Why does the wind sound so lonely? Aunt Zonie said Navajos believe that life is breathed into body by the wind.

And she has told me the story of the origin of First Woman, how "raising her skirt she had looked at her parts and the sun struck her vagina and sent a thrill through her, and she became pregnant and gave birth to a being that the winds picked up. And in time this being developed into the lonely traveling big Yei."

A traveling wind. But the wind will stay, it has always been present on earth, will be here through eternity. But for man, just as there was a beginning, there will also be an ending.

A star comes out and then the tens of thousands that you can never count, never measure, never know their beginning, their ending.

Evening: Aunt Zonie and I sit in the darkness, with only the glow of the wood-burning iron stove. I have cooked the evening meal, mutton stew, and now I want to wash the pots and pans, but "No, daughter, just leave them until the morning." Do it now, do it now. My old training is difficult to forget, but Zonie knows it will all be the same in the next hundred years.

She rummages through boxes kept under the eaves of the hogan and finds her collection of battered, torn photographs. She uses a flashlight to focus on the obscure memories of the past.

"I hate to tell you, my dear . . ." and a great sadness comes over her. She sighs a kind of moan, that mother moan for a lost one who was all joy, all tragedy. A girl, her first child, died of pneumonia; and then the second child, a boy—is she saying that he was crushed under a horse? I can hardly hear, her voice has grown inaudible with sadness. Then it was ten years before she gave birth to Dolly.

Now here's Dolly, grown up. A schoolteacher. With a high-rise wiglet. High-heel shoes. She looks like an Anglo. Yet she proudly wears Zonie's turquoise necklace. Zonie has given away all her prized possessions. And she is now as she began in this world—with her bare hands.

* * *

I worry about Zonie's cold and drive her to the Fort Defiance hospital. When we walk up to the registration desk, a Navajo woman, in her twenties with an Anglo hairstyle, looks to me to speak for Zonie. "May I help you?" she asks, in English. I say nothing and eventually she speaks in Navajo with Aunt Zonie, and arranges an appointment.

After Zonie's name is called, I sit in the lobby, among the Navajos, awaiting her return.

About thirty minutes elapse and Zonie comes out with a bright face. The Anglo doctor has given her some pills, and told her, as Zonie now relates to me, "Grandmother, you'll live to be one hundred!"

As we go out, I ask: was she hungry?

And she nods affirmatively.

We first go by the Fort Defiance trading post, and the white owner gives Zonie a message from her daughter Dolly. Dolly, who has a husband and children, wants her mother to come to their home in Tohatchi.

Is anything wrong? I ask Zonie.

"No, she just wants me to baby-sit," Zonie replies.

We go into a small cafe, and Zonie orders the Anglo specialities: hamburger, malted milk, apple pie. She can't be feeling bad with that kind of appetite! She is like my mother: feminine, younger than me in her zest, her little-girl outlook on life.

As we are sitting, Zonie nods to another Navajo woman, wrapped in a blanket, also in her seventies. I suggest we invite her to our table. The woman gladly accepts; I watch the two women, gossiping in Navajo, as pleased as children at a party.

I ask Zonie if our companion lives alone in a hogan.

"She lives in a hogan, with her son," Zonie tells me.

Since the old woman does not speak English, I ask: might I visit her and have her son interpret for us?

"No, the son does not speak English," Zonie relays the woman's words. "He's never been to school in his life."

I ask: how old is he?

"Thirty-six."

And never been to school? And never married?

"Once he went away, years ago, and got married. But he came back without his clothes. His wife had fought with him, scratched him, torn up all his clothes, and now the son is afraid of women."

The mother somehow seemed very pleased about that.

The next day, I drive Zonie to her daughter's home in Tohatchi, northeast of Window Rock. Dolly lives in a spacious home with carpeting.

As we three women sit in overstuffed comfortable lounging chairs, Dolly tells about going, as a young girl, on a "Y" trip, sponsored by the Young Women's Christian Association: "I met a Spanish girl and I knew her language was Spanish and then I met a black girl, and I asked, 'And what is your language?' And the black girl replied, 'English.'" Dolly stops a moment, and then adds, "And I felt so sorry for her. She did not have a culture."

After embracing Zonie, I leave to drive back to Window Rock.

As I drive I reflect on Dolly's remarks. She is typical of many Indians whose white schoolteachers have somehow implied that black is not as good as white or red. But do "educated" Indians think they are inferior? One Navajo woman, telling of a young girl's funeral, said: "She looked *so pretty,* you couldn't tell she was a Navajo."

I am staying now in a trailer home that is owned by Sara Begay who works in a program to aid Navajo alcoholics. Through Sara, I have become friends with an older sister, Evelyn Silentman, who is a secretary in the Bureau of Indian Affairs in Window Rock.

Sara is reed-slim, while Evelyn is more typically Navajo, just over five feet, squat and sturdy. She has a broad Mongolian face, and shoulder-length gray hair with waves that suggest she has some Anglo blood, inasmuch as the Indians have straight hair.

Whenever I have seen Evelyn sitting behind her modern steel and chrome desk with the punch-button extension phones and her IBM typewriter, she has insistently talked to me not about what was "new," but what was "old," as if compelled to stress her Indian-ness. Once she showed me an old turquoise ring, and another time, an old straw basket used in healing ceremonials. She always seems intent on bridging two cultures, and I suspect that she labors under a strain as she constantly juggles the demands of her two worlds, Indian and white.

I invite the two sisters to lunch. I first get Sara at her Fort Defiance office—housed, like many offices, in a trailer —and then we go to the BIA in Window Rock for Evelyn. We drive some miles west to a white man's trailer cafe, the kind where mama's in the kitchen heating packaged frozen apple pie and papa is frying hamburgers. When we enter I notice that the customers are half and half, Anglos and Navajos, and all are eating the speciality of the house,

a hamburger known as a "Hungry Indian." The mobile
trailer stands in the vast emptiness of the sandy windswept
desert like a permanent eyesore.

The trailer cafe is one of the three "in" places to have
lunch, all of them run by whites. As we munch on tasteless
hamburgers, I ponder the influence the whites have, especially in Sara's life: she lives, works, now eats in a trailer.

After lunch, as we drive back to the BIA building,
Evelyn, who sits in the back seat, begins telling Sara that
she wants to go back home to Piñon to arrange a "meeting," that she has stepped on a snake. I understand her
mixture of Navajo-English words, but am puzzled by her
references to a "meeting" and a malady caused by stepping
on a snake. I glance in the rear-view mirror, and Evelyn
suddenly looks enlarged and agitated, a woman unburden-
ing herself of some strange secret.

Only minutes before, Evelyn had been in the world of
the here and now, and not an Indian at all. She was like
any other secretary who punches time clocks and goes out
to lunch and orders a hamburger and apple pie, and wears
a "miracle" wash-and-wear fabric and works for a white
boss who gives her too much typing and migraine head-
aches. Now she seems privately bewitched.

I drive on to the BIA, and Evelyn gets out and says
nothing. Navajos, unlike Anglos, do not express gratitude,
or indulge in trite amenities, such as "say, that was a swell
meal," or "it was really nice of you," or even, "see you
later." Our luncheon excursion over, she simply leaves.

Sara seems deeply concerned, as I might be had my
sister announced that a doctor had told her she had cancer.
I want to blurt out to Sara: this is ridiculous; we both
know Evelyn walks around on concrete all day, and how
can she have stepped on a snake? Eventually I ask Sara:
did she say she was having "sinking spells"? When Sara

does not respond, I ask point-blank: what's wrong with her?

"*Tah honeesgai*—she feels sick all over," Sara replies. "We Navajos do not define what ails us the way you do. We do not specify one part of us, and say—'My head hurts,' or 'My stomach aches.' It's not our custom to separate the 'head' from the 'body.'

"The *hatali*, the chanter or singer or what you call our Medicine Man, recommends the proper *hatal*, a sacred song or chant, a certain Sing as we say. This will be the right ceremony to eradicate the *cause* of the sickness.

"In the ceremony itself, the Medicine Man treats the person, the entire person—and not the sickness."

She adds that all ceremonies are of extraordinary complexity, extending one, three, five or nine nights, with hundreds of prayers recited, and songs chanted.

We drive to Fort Defiance, where I deposit Sara at her office, and as I start back to Window Rock I speculate that our white doctors have become such specialists in the treatment of maladies that they often forget *you*, the person. Anglos even joke about an operation's being a success, "except the patient died." Sara's emphasis on the Medicine Man's treating the person as a whole, inseparable organism impresses me. Still, is her religion one of faith or one of fear?

Navajo commandments—to avoid snakes, lightning-struck trees, bears and coyotes—all seem based on fears. Jung observed that civilized man regards himself naturally as immeasurably above these things. Still, I know "civilized" friends who fear cats crossing their paths, and offices or apartments on any thirteenth floor.

In my city life I have no trouble avoiding lightning-struck trees, coyotes, bears and snakes, but here in Navajoland they are everyday dangers. I have heard of several persons killed by lightning. And coyotes and snakes also kill people and sheep. But Sara said, "People should not kill snakes, just avoid them."

I reason that snakes might do some good; they kill prairie dogs that are destructive to grazing lands. Only in this light—of the snakes' being useful—can I see why they should live. The Navajos, obviously, have other reasons.

But how had Evelyn inadvertently "stepped on a snake"? And was one to believe she had actually stepped on the snake, or perhaps just on his shadow? While the cause of her malady does not make sense to me, she is luckier in some ways than the Anglo who might feel "sick all over" and have nothing on which to blame his malady. Now Evelyn at least has an explanation—any answer at times seeming better than no answer—and a ritual that will no doubt leave her feeling better.

Arrangements are made for Evelyn to go to her parents' home in Piñon in a few days. And Sara and I will drive there together on Saturday for the final day of the three-day Sing.

Early morning: Sara and I drive west past Ganado and turn north. On our long, lonely journey Sara talks about how poor they were—she and Evelyn were two of ten children—and how they had been sent to various church mission schools, "because they were free.

"I attended a Catholic mission school, also Baptist and Mormon schools. Many of your church groups come here to help the poor, 'pagan' Indians, and many end up doing more harm than good. There are countless instances of Navajos being baptized many times in different religions, I was one of these. I tried many different Anglo religions, yet I still retained my Navajo ways, my belief in the curing ceremonials, the Medicine Man—*my* religion."

I refrain from asking: what is your religion? That would be the same as asking: what is your life?

Our reformation divided the world into two arenas: church and state. The morality of one was not necessarily related to the morality of the other. Thus, we whites live in a secular, compartmentalized world, best exemplified perhaps by the southern Christian who could pray on Sunday and lynch on Monday. We may worship on Easter or Yom Kippur, and we may solemnize birth, marriage and death, but most of us are too busy for our religion, although for questionnaire purposes we can usually identify it as Protestant, Catholic, Hebrew, agnostic, atheist.

What about Evelyn? I ask Sara. Did she also go to schools established by whites?

"Yes, several," Sara replies. "And then she was adopted by a Mormon family and converted to that faith."

The Mormons are among the busiest proselytizers on the reservation. Many families in Utah adopt Indian children and change them into "white" Mormons. While some blacks have charged the Mormons are discriminatory—no black can become an elder in the Mormon church—the Indians have been placed outside the Mormons' concept of "colored" by classification as descendants of the lost tribe of Israel.

Sara continues: "Evelyn stayed only one year with the Mormon family, and returned to the reservation. At nineteen, she married a Navajo who had converted to Christianity—he was a Baptist. And Evelyn joined him in that church.

"But her husband—he rode broncs in rodeos—was a heavy drinker. Evelyn stuck with him. They had three children. But he continued to drink heavily and he often beat her and the children. In time, he left Evelyn and lived with a younger, prettier woman. One day he shot and killed this younger woman and was sent to a penitentiary for life. Now he writes to Evelyn and wants her to allow the children to write him, and she does."

I think of Evelyn's white boss whom I've often heard ridicule Navajo ways, and her husband—and what had been the pressures on him! Raised in white people's schools and churches, a Navajo must find it difficult to retain his identity.

How did she manage? I ask Sara.

"I have joined the Native American Church," she tells me. "I find a greater sense of preserving my human values, as a Navajo, in this faith."

As we continue our drive, I have the sensation of being borne through space; a feeling akin to drifting on a parachute, skiing down a mountain, floating in a glider, land and sky encompassing me, no other moving vehicles in front or behind or on either side, alone in a placid void. My reverie is abruptly ended as Sara, holding her neck, begins to make strange, frantic hand signals. Her face is drained of color. She seems to be choking. I pull off the road, and she stumble out of the car in a near-faint, gasping for air.

Not quite knowing what to do, and thinking that Sara has been frightened or shocked, I look on the floor of the car for a snake, or some simple explanation for the sudden attack. I see nothing. I get out from behind the wheel and walk to her side but do nothing more than stand there, somewhat certain that she had brought the attack on herself. After much fanning of her face, the coughing subsides. Sara indicates she is all right and she gets back in the car.

We drive on silently. I know Sara will explain in her own time. After some minutes she tells me: "I've had these choking spells. I got too close to a tree that had been struck by lightning."

I would have guessed any reason but that one. Still, I once had an aunt who claimed she got choking spells when she didn't go to church on Sundays—the Methodist church. But why, I ask Sara, did she blame a lightning-struck tree?

"I saw a Hand Trembler yesterday and he explained what had happened."

I had heard about the Hand Trembler, sometimes called a Hand Shaker or Star Gazer; he seemed to go into a trance to learn his secrets. Perhaps he was like a hypnotist who places himself, rather than the patient, in a trance. But I am curious how his role differs from the Medicine Man's in allaying fears that even among the most educated, most enlightened Navajos, such as Evelyn and Sara, seem to be as common as the bread they eat.

How, I inquire, did the Hand Trembler know she had touched a lightning-struck tree? I couldn't imagine how he knew if Sara didn't know. But she is patient with me, and explains:

"He knows because he has the spirit of the Gila Monster; it's the spirit that tells him what's wrong with a person. The Gila Monster causes his hand to shake, and then the hand 'divines' or tells him the nature of your illness. He's what you'd call a diagnostician. He never treats you, he discovers the *cause* of your sickness."

I ask Sara: after the Hand Trembler told her the *cause* of her ailment, what had he recommended?

"A ceremony we call the Evil Way," she says, adding that while she's in Piñon for Evelyn's cure, she will talk with the Medicine Man and arrange another Sing, to be held in a month or so.

It is difficult for me to appreciate Sara's faith in the Sings without knowing more about the Navajo myths and legends. But I have heard enough to know that the Navajo myths, like those in the Old Testament, tell exactly how the world came into being, how the first people became afflicted and how they obtained supernatural help for their maladies. Evelyn and Sara and other Navajos are following the examples of The People, as related in the old myths. Far from being fantasies, myths are derived by extremely "logical" minds who desire to make the world intelligible.

I try to visualize Evelyn and Sara as children, with their eight brothers and sisters and their mother and father on a winter's night. They are on their sheepskins, sprawled out on the dirt floor; the hogan is dark except for the blaze of a fire, and they are all huddled around that fire. None of them would have ever seen a movie or TV, they did not have books or magazines, they had only an oral tradition to transmit their histories, their legends.

When I ask Sara to tell me the story of the beginning of the Navajos, she relates the tale much as she might have heard it as a child:

"Life began in a series of places far beneath the surface of the earth, and The People came through the Black World, the Red World and the Blue World—and, when the present world was rid of its monsters and flooding waters —The People emerged to this world's surface.

"And First Man and First Woman," she says, 'were created from two perfect ears of corn."

Corn has always meant the difference between life and death to Indians. First grown by the Indians, it is the supreme achievement in plant domestication. Of the three great world cereals, Oriental rice, European wheat and American corn, the indigenous New World plant is the most nutritious, versatile and valuable crop today. It therefore seems logical that this "gift of life" might be said to have created First Man and First Woman.

One aspect of Sara's Navajo religion I find difficult to

comprehend is that there's no concept of sin, and their ritual is not concerned with morality. The dual elements of good and evil are always present. For instance, Sara explains that First Man and First Woman, who had supernatural powers for doing good, also had supernatural powers for evil.

"Because of them, it's very easy to become bewitched," Sara says.

Bewitched, I ask, by a ghost?

"No, not by a ghost, by a witch. They're not the same at all. A ghost is what is left of a dead person, the 'good' goes on, the 'evil' part stays here. First Man and First Woman began Witchery Way. They ground up flesh from dead people and made a 'corpse poison'—it looks like pollen, and it can be dropped into a hogan from the smokehole, or placed in your nose or mouth while you're sleeping or blown through a stick into your face.

"Witches today dress up in the hides of animals, like a coyote or a wolf. They roam at night and that's why a Navajo does not like to leave his hogan at night. As a child, I heard a lot about were-animals. And sometimes I'd wonder: how can a full grown man get himself into the hide of a wolf or coyote? I had seen dried animal skins and I couldn't figure how a man got into such dry skin. It was all quite a miracle. Sometimes witches use 'corpse poison,' but they only can shoot you with other objects—arrows or maybe a stone, quill or piece of charcoal. And they can easily shoot you without your being aware of it."

Sara's grave face indicates that her thoughts still dwell on how easily one might be shot by a witch.

Had she, I ask, been shot by a witch?

"Yes," she replies. "When I was a child, my mother took me to a Sing, and then I didn't feel well, and I lost my sight. But at first, we didn't know where or how it happened. So my mother called in the Hand Trembler. He sits

beside you and rubs corn pollen on your feet, knees, palms
of your hands, breast, between your shoulders, on top of
your head and he puts the pollen on his arm and prays to
the Gila Monster: *I want you to tell me what is wrong
with her.*

"Then he 'listens' and his hand and arm begin to shake
and he gets his message from the way his hand moves. He
said that when I was at this ceremony, a witch had shot an
arrow into my skull, and he prescribed a Sucking ceremony
so that the object could be sucked out of my head. Then
we got a Medicine Man and asked him to perform this
ceremony, and he sucked a small arrowhead and some pus
out—it was back of my eyes"—and Sara points to a spot on
her left forehead.

Was the skin broken? I ask.

"No, but the arrowhead and the pus just came out when
he was sucking and then he spit them out of his mouth.
And there was some blood in there, too. And then I was
not blind anymore, and later I was tested and I had
twenty-twenty vision."

From Sara's face I discern she's convinced that the
Medicine Man did indeed suck out the arrowhead that a
witch had shot into her.

"My mother wanted me to be a Hand Trembler," Sara
continues. "She thought I had that power. To be a Medicine Man or Medicine Woman, you have to study, to learn
many songs. There are over five hundred songs in the
Night Chant alone. But to be a Hand Trembler, that's a
gift.

"The Gila Monster has to 'accept' you and then you can
listen to his messages but the reason the Gila Monster
didn't accept me was that as a child I was bitten on my
arm by a rabbit."

*   *   *

We are now driving through brilliant badlands of such length and breadth that no western movie ever captured their amplitude. When we pass red and gray clays and logs of yellow and red petrified wood, Sara says, "Those are the bones of Big Monster." The land was once luxuriant with vegetation and with dinosaurs and other strange reptiles wandering about. For the Indians who retain a sense of awe and wonder in their everyday life, the Big Monsters never really left the world.

Before reaching Chinle, entrance to the beautiful Canyon de Chelly National Monument, we turn west and drive through what seems like an endless vastness.

After a three-hour drive, we reach Piñon and drive to the Silentman residence. Sara has explained that the family now lives in a modest frame house, but that they have retained the hogan for Sings. She tells me that Evelyn and their mother and women relatives will now be gathered in the frame house to enjoy a big meal.

As we get out of the car and walk past the hogan to the frame house, Sara remarks, "We've come a long way." And I presume she refers to their moving from a dirt floor house to one with a wooden floor. Their "modern" house even appears to be equipped with electricity. Entering the kitchen door, I see a woman who welcomes me with her eyes, Ida Silentman. She is the mother, kneading dough, slapping it between the palms of her hands. Her eyes linger, very young eyes in an unwrinkled face.

A half dozen women, among them Evelyn, are sitting on the floor, and I feel a surge of Anglo disgust, which evokes so much of what I have heard from white critics: How can you teach *these people?* Get them off the floor and turn your back, and they're right back where they were, on the floor; give them a washtub to boil their dirty clothes, and look—they've filled it with greasy mutton! The women have surrounded the washtub like vultures around some dead carcass, and they are sensuously—and in an

Anglo's eyes, revoltingly—eating with their hands, although it is less like eating than *feeding*, animal-like, from a trough.

A Navajo once told me, "I've seen Anglos get sick and vomit from watching Navajos eat mutton."

And most revolting to me at this moment is Evelyn, of all people, she who knows how to run the IBM machine and wear modern dresses—sitting cross-legged in a long, fluted, six-yards-wide velveteen skirt and satin blouse, loaded down with heavy turquoise jewelry, looking like some ancient imperial potentate's wife whose worth might be measured by the pound.

"Food is a very important part of the ceremonial. You have to have lots of mutton to give a Sing," Sara tells me.

We are still standing by the door when one of the old women with more lines in her face than a road map nods towards me and, speaking in Navajo which Sara translates, asks: "Is she one of these 'dainty' Anglos?"

"No," Sara responds, "she likes to sit on the floor. And she likes mutton."

Sara and I walk over and join the circle of women. I know what is expected of me and what I myself desire—to dive into their affections, to be one among them. I have often eaten while sitting on *klang* floors with Korean women. And I have sopped up turtle and monkey soup along the Amazon. I recall one old Indian in the Amazonian jungle asking another, "Doesn't she speak?" meaning doesn't she talk our tongue, and the Brazilian jungle dweller, my host, replying, "No, but she eats *anything*."

With Sara's words as a challenge, I eagerly demonstrate a Gargantuan appetite by picking up a large chunk of fry bread from the floor to dip into the washtub and "spoon" out the mutton. Then I realize it's more than I can chew, if in fact I can even get it in my mouth. But there's no retreat, for it would be an admission that the old woman

was right, that I was "one of those 'dainty' Anglos" after
all. Once I put the chunk in my mouth I know that only a
diamond drilling bit could pierce it. I take a deep breath
and swallow it whole, confident that my cast-iron stomach
is equal to the challenge of digesting it.

The woman on my right, I learn, is the wife of the
Medicine Man, Kee Preston, whose Navajo name is Blue
Goat. She has five children and is expecting another in a
couple of months, although her multi-layered skirts con-
ceal her pregnancy. She has a childlike innocent face, and
intrigues me by chewing gum and somehow eating food
at the same time. She shows me a purse and indicates her
"grandmother" made it. The "grandmother" is an elderly
woman who wears a black satin skirt, long pendants in her
pierced ears and a made-in-Pendleton, Oregon, blanket
wrapped around her.

After Sara and I have sat for an hour with Evelyn and
the clan, we get up to stretch our legs. I inspect the
framed pictures of Jesus Christ hanging on the walls,
among them Leonardo's famous scene of the Last Supper.
And I see that the Twenty-third Psalm, "The Lord Is My
Shepherd," has been framed, and prominently displayed.

This family seems to have easily reconciled the "truths"
expressed by the teachings of Jesus Christ and by their
own Medicine Man.

Leaving the frame house, Sara and I walk a few steps,
back to the windowless, dome-roofed mud-adobe hut that
traditionally has served the Navajo as home and "church."
Navajos have no formal meeting place for religious practices; their "religion" simply exists in every person, in
every family, in every part of their land, unorganized,
private and deeply felt.

I am deeply impressed by this faith. I want to be a part
of this religion, to throw myself into the Navajo mold, and
yet I look down at Sara's old shoes and remember she had

asked if maybe I had some old shoes that would fit her.
My ethic equates good morality with a good pair of shoes.
I fear I might have been one of the first to reject the
teachings of Christ, had I seen him in his "hippie"
hair and attire. The substantial citizens of Imperial Rome
and the Orthodox Jews of the synagogue looked down on
the fishermen, beggars and the prostitutes who followed
Jesus. And more recently dollars seem next to Godliness:
J. P. Morgan took entire trainloads of Episcopalians to
conventions, John D. Rockefeller had his Baptist adviser
helping him distribute his wealth, and Richard Nixon
invited Billy Graham to the White House.

Just before we enter the hogan, Sara explains that the
Medicine Man and his assistants are putting the finishing
touches on a sand painting that depicts "Holy People"
who can journey to the other world for Evelyn, intercede
for her, put her world back in harmony with nature.

"You want to take a peek at the sand painting?" Sara
asks. When I nod a Yes, she lifts a blanket "door" and I
gaze at a rigidly stylized abstraction of strikingly original
design, with brilliant yellows and blues, as well as whites
and blacks. Two elongated bodies, one with a square head,
the other with a round head, stand erect, facing toward
the east, the direction of the sun and all good spiritual
things. There is no background to the design; it is executed
directly on the dirt floor. Beyond the sand painting in
the rear of the hogan stands Kee Preston, the Medicine
Man. He is a sturdy figure in his thirties who wears tight
khaki-colored work pants and a shocking-pink short-
sleeved knitted sports shirt. Singers or Medicine Men
always dress as simply as other Navajos, as a richly attired
Medicine Man might be accused of being more interested
in money than in his patients.

He and I exchange glances that seem to acknowledge
I have crossed into another culture which both of us

understand to be vastly different from my own. He knows my white world. Sara has told me he once worked in an aircraft assembly plant in California, and now is back home. One in every three Navajos who leave the reservation comes back, as it were, to the wellsprings of his culture, to the dirt floor of the hogan.

Speaking in Navajo, but with tone and gestures I understand, the Medicine Man is saying:

"You can't just stand there and observe, you must participate, you must contribute to the painting. You are no stranger, not an outsider looking in, come in, make yourself at home, we are all here to work together, to pray together, we—and the gods—must cure Evelyn."

I open my right hand and he pours crushed stone pellets into my palm. And he shows me how to "draw" by letting the colored pigments trickle slowly between thumb and forefinger onto the dirt floor. As I "draw" I see that the abstraction is perfectly symmetrical. Four sets of feathers, with twelve feathers to a set, enclose the composition that has taken him and two assistants four hours to complete.

Did he himself, I ask the Medicine Man, create the design?

"No, I have the image in my head. It's been handed down in memory from one Singer to another. And there are more than five hundred patterns."

In addition to memorizing sand paintings patterns, Kee Preston must learn by rote hundreds of chants and songs, perfecting not only the words but the nuances of their healing symbolism. Learning one Sing is equivalent to learning the score of a Wagnerian opera.

My eyes still on the painting, I ask Preston: Who are these Holy People?

"They know how to deal with supernatural forces. When you speak of 'holy' you mean someone morally perfect, *good*. When we talk about 'holy' we mean those who are powerful, mysterious, sacred, not profane." He adds, "The painting is important because Evelyn can see, can touch these figures."

Like a medieval glass painting, this pattern makes visible and concrete religious concepts that otherwise are nebulous. But unlike the windows, this painting is temporary, a fugitive link between the Navajo and his gods, to be erased once the Sing is finished.

To an Anglo, this is a quaint, fetching fantasy, a communication etched in sand, not marble, and as frail as a mound of dust in a high wind. One moment to see the gods, and then back to the nothingness of a bare dirt floor.

Sara and I step outside, where Evelyn and her parents, relatives and friends have gathered to move into the hogan. There are about thirty altogether, including several children, and as they go in, I wonder how the small room will accommodate us all. Sara and I follow the others and sit on the dirt floor, just to the left of the blanket door.

We are in position, against the walls of the hogan. All of us on the earth, except Evelyn, who sits on stacks of folded blankets and yards of piece goods that will be given the Medicine Man. In addition, he will be paid ten dollars for each day's services.

The wife of the Medicine Man, her childlike, unlined face placid except for the movement of her bubble gum, sits to the right of the door, as do all of the women; while the men are to the left—and among these four old men, the chorus, start their musical prayers, the singing and chanting interrupted only when they pause to clear their throats with a loud rasping noise. Their voices leap back and forth between octaves with impressive virtuosity. The leader, with a headband and no teeth, wears a huge robin's-egg-blue turquoise ring. "He has three wives," Sara whispers, and then explains that all of the chants stress purification, and that the Medicine Man, the chanters, Evelyn, all participants must forego sex during the days of a Sing.

When my eyes turn back to Evelyn, I am amazed to see the Medicine Man standing over her, chanting, and helping her to undress. Off come the bracelets and rings and the long, heavy strands of turquoise necklaces; then the Medicine Man helps Evelyn remove her overblouse. Now Evelyn sits exposed, and I see ugly breasts hanging like two empty hot-water bottles, and I feel that we are all committing some breach of decorum, engaging in some arcane exhibition, not so much holy as simply obscene.

I have seen beautiful, young naked women in stage shows in Paris and in New York, and I was not dismayed as I am now. Perhaps I felt this way because in my culture an older woman's exposed body is repulsive, that the reach for some holy contact seems defiled by an older woman's nakedness. It takes me a while to accept that the Navajos see nothing obscene or blasphemous about Evelyn's bare breasts, feel no embarrassment because age has disfigured her.

Evelyn removes all her clothes except her skirt, which she pulls up to her knees; for her this disrobing is probably no different from the average Anglo woman's undressing before an assortment of doctors and nurses.

Now the Medicine Man draws the pattern of a necklace hanging low on Evelyn's chest, executing much of his painting directly on her caved-in breasts. He moves to her outstretched legs and paints snakes on her feet.

The old sagacious lead man in the chorus tells the Medicine Man (as Sara translates it for me): "You forgot the snake's *tongue*," and the people relax and chuckle. The Medicine Man paints the snake's tongue on Evelyn's toenail.

The Navajo shaman leads Evelyn to a pile of coals that one of his assistants has placed directly in front of me. "The smoke will carry away the evil spirits," Sara explains.

He directs her back to the stylized gods who can carry messages for her, and she sits down directly on top of the sand painting. "This enables her to get in close contact with the 'Holy People,'" Sara whispers. "The chanting has awakened the spirits, now Evelyn can commune with the spirits." I study Evelyn's face and see nothing to indicate she's suffused by a spiritual glow or a holy spirit. A dreary sameness marks her face.

The Medicine Man touches Evelyn's feet, praying in a Navajo singsong that Sara interprets:

"*May her feet be well, her feet restore unto her.*" And he presses his hands upon her hands—"her hands restore unto her. . . ." And he touches almost every part of her body, her shoulders, breasts, back, head.

The scene reminds me of the stories of my childhood that recounted how a healing touch—with prayers—could save. "Your father was dying of pneumonia and his brother Oscar sat up with him all night, and *held his hand.*" My father later claimed that "healing touch" had saved his life.

I watch the Medicine Man take portions of corn mush from a sacred basket and feed Evelyn, placing the mush on her tongue. He anoints Evelyn with holy water and gives her sips of medicated brew. An assistant passes a community cup of medicated brew, and I take the cup and sip the milky substance; and then—as others have done—I spit it out in the palms of my hands and rub it over my face, arms, breasts and hands to cleanse myself.

"It is holy water," Sara tells me, but when I taste I lack the faith to accept its holiness. Yet as a child I drank a purplish substance at Christian communion services, believing it was "the blood of Christ."

The on-going singing and chanting, based on rhythm rather than melody, and dissonant to my Anglo ears, the mesmerizing power in the gourd rattles, and the disfigured Evelyn before me—all of the sights and sounds leave me dizzily uncertain as to who or where I am. The mystical, the intuitive can never be rationally apprehended.

If only I could *see* some miracle, rather than try to experience it within. Then I could judge this "holy" man in the shocking-pink knitted shirt and tight work pants. Evelyn sits grotesquely besmeared—the coal dust and burnt orange and black pollen giving her the appearance of a gaudy derelict who might have been salvaged from some urban alley.

I feel transported back a thousand years in time, a witness to a ritual as repulsive as it is primitive. My mind conjures up old prints of aborigines wallowing in the mud as if divinely inspired. But then I reflect on our "strange" customs of dunking people into streams to "purify" them.

Was it "primitive" for Evelyn to be anointed by holy water, but not "primitive" for me to be baptized in the name of the Father-the Son-and-the Holy Ghost, the Christians' three-in-one that we all explain and none of us understands? And would Evelyn be better off with the white people's astrology, numerology, and predictions by Jeane Dixon? Given a choice among reality therapy, Billy Graham, Tarot cards, and your average psychiatrist, wouldn't Evelyn deem herself "logical" to choose Kee Preston?

After more than two hours of the singing, chanting, praying, Preston hands Evelyn's jewelry back to her, and gives her an additional "necklace"—one made of evergreen sprigs, symbol of everlasting life. She returns to her original position, on the blankets, and she puts on her overblouse, her stockings, shoes.

Finally the Medicine Man picks up a feathered stick

and, still chanting, destroys the painting, from the center outward, in the order in which it had been made. A few seconds later no sign of the beautiful pattern remains. "All evidence of the painting must be destroyed before dark," Sara tells me. "Otherwise the evil spirits of the night might be attracted and come to earth to harm someone."

The Sing is over, everyone stumbles out into the sunshine. They seem to be relieved that the ceremony has now been concluded. And many already are preparing to leave for the journey back to their homes.

Each person seems concerned with his own immediate plans. But what about Evelyn? Is she cured?

Sara explains, "She must leave the painting on her body for four days before she washes it off. The cure takes place during this period."

I do not doubt that the Medicine Man performs his own kind of "miracles," because the Navajos believe he does. They report "cures," and they are comforted and relieved by his work. Their faith is a restorative. It might be argued that the Medicine Man practices psychosomatic medicine, in the modern sense, by "treating" the person as a whole, an inseparable organism, blending an ancient workable psychology with the myths of divine belief. From the very beginning Sara stressed that the Medicine Man would treat Evelyn as a person—not just a malady.

I recall that one old Navajo had been asked why he went to a Medicine Man instead of white doctors. He explained:

"You go to a hospital and maybe once a day the doctor comes around and he stays about five minutes, and he asks you some questions. Maybe he gives you a little medicine. About the only thing they do is put something in your mouth, and see how hot you are. The rest of the time you just lie there. But the Medicine Man helps you all the time—he gives you lots of medicine and he sings all night. He does lots of things all over your body, all of your body is treated."

Part III

BESSIE YELLOWHAIR

Evelyn Silentman introduced me to a clan cousin, twenty-four-year-old Bessie Yellowhair. Bessie is bright-eyed, enthusiastic, energetic, with a sturdy, straight, ample body, not fat but strong, all the joints and parts moving with Rolex precision. She is me as I remember me, determined to find myself, determined to hold on to my family, my traditions, to use them, to grow up from them, as the tree uses its roots.

Indians are supposedly not materialistic, but Navajos seem very impressed when Bessie drives around in her own pickup truck, which in prestige value is equivalent to an Anglo's Cadillac. When I first met Bessie, I studied her features to determine why I found her attractive. Her features are not perfect. But beauty is always short of perfection, never symmetrical, finished. Just as one wishes to turn up the curved-down mouth of the beauty, Lucrezia Crivelli, in the classic Leonardo painting, so I think of turning up the nose of Bessie Yellowhair. But an innate beauty overcomes her subtle flaws, the raw, unfinished edges of an almost perfect picture.

Most Navajos have stepped into the "mainstream" that eventually will wash away all their Indian-ness, and while many older Navajos have only gingerly tested the waters, Bessie appears to be waist-deep in them.

Bessie's parents live in a hogan about forty miles out from Tuba City, Arizona. Bessie goes there often, but she lives with a sister, Lucy, in a small house midway between Steamboat trading post and Ganado. Lucy, whose husband works for the railroad in California, is in her early thirties, and has never worked outside the home. Bessie, who has on occasion taken jobs off the reservation, now works as a ward clerk in the forty-five bed Ganado hospital run by Project Hope, the worldwide medical training and treatment program.

When Bessie and I go to visit her parents, I see how easily Bessie bridges two cultures, stepping from her pickup truck into the dirt floor hogan, and sitting on the floor, beside her mother Harriet, who speaks no English.

At length Mrs. Yellowhair rises, and stokes the wood in the iron stove, setting to work making fry bread. Almost eternally, it must seem to her, she has done this. People come in, they have been traveling, they are hungry.

When the mother places the hot fluffy morsels of fry bread before Bessie and me, she again sits with us, and I ask Bessie to tell me about her mother's marriage.

"She was chosen by my father's family. The marriage was arranged in one day," Bessie says. "His family had to give eight horses and some jewelry and some money for her. Our custom is different from the old Anglo practice of giving a dowry with the girl.

"All of us were born in the hogan. There was another baby between Mary and me; but at the time I didn't know Mother was pregnant, she kept moving around one night, and she had a miscarriage. In the morning when I got up I found some blood . . . my father was away. My mother had to do it all herself.

"I remember very well when Mary—she lives in Phoenix now—was born. I had come in from herding sheep. And my mother was in pain. She said, 'Run up to your grandmother's'—at that time, my grandmother lived in a hogan near Mid Mesa—so I ran the six miles over there, and told her that my mom was sick. So my grandfather saddled his horse, and we took off running back to the house, and

Grandmother followed in her wagon. In a few hours there were a lot of people here. And my grandfather brought the Medicine Man in. Because my mother was having pain and she was ready to deliver.

"They had dug a small hole and tied a rope from a stake to the ceiling, and my mother was holding onto the rope. They got her over the hole, and she sat there—and then all of a sudden, people laughed, and I knew that the baby had been delivered. When I came in, they were washing the little baby, and my mother looked so fine, and she smiled, and everybody was so happy about it, and there was a lot of people in there. My uncle had delivered the baby and my aunt had helped—and the hogan was so crowded, everybody had helped—they wrapped the baby in sheepskin.

"My mother didn't stay lying down, she was up and around, that same day," Bessie continues.

"When my brother Bert was born, my father was attending a Yeibeichei dance. He didn't think my mother was going to deliver that morning. But just when the sun came up, she started labor. No one was home except my sister Rosemary. She ran to my grandmother's—but no one was there. And she went all the way to Steamboat trying to get someone to help my mother. But she couldn't find anyone. By the time she got back, my mother already had delivered, she did everything herself."

I ask Bessie if her mother gave her one of the Navajo Sing-ceremonials called the Blessing Way when she had her first menstrual period. This Sing is given on different occasions such as the blessing of a new home, and also on the occasion of a girl reaching womanhood.

"Yes. I had that," Bessie says. "And all of my sisters. It is beautiful time for us." It was a beautiful time for Bessie, because she had been taught that way. However, the menstrual experience for me, ignorant and unprepared, was shameful. My mother and my older sisters, feeling the taboo of not discussing a matter of blood, had never told me what to expect. If I have come to find the customs of the Navajos strange and different, what would Bessie think in exploring my past, my culture, my first menstrual period? Surely, no less strange and perhaps even more bizarre and inexplicable.

Was the Blessing Way ceremony important? I ask.

"It is important not only because you are going to become a woman, but it teaches you to become a good person—not only for yourself but for your family and clan."

Bessie, wanting to return to Ganado before dark, leaves the hogan. And I will stay. She goes to a world of telephones and electricity, and I stay behind, in her "yesterday" world.

Living with the Yellowhair family, I have begun to see that sheep occupy a strategic, social and economic role in their lives. You might say that what coal is to a Pennsylvania or West Virginia family and wheat to a Kansan, sheep are to a Navajo. Sheep represent a source of food, clothing, revenue.

And, although the Navajos have not always lived by sheep-raising—it has come about only within the past 400 years—they now feel that sheep have always been the basis of their economy. The emotional and prestige value of sheep is so deeply embedded in their psyche that they refuse to see that an overpopulation of sheep has undoubtedly contributed not only to the destruction of grass but also, through nature's inevitable interrelations, to the destruction of the soil and depletion of the water supplies on which the grass depends.

Among those of us living in the hogan are three of the Yellowhairs' ten children: Rosemary (with her children),

Bert, and the youngest of the Yellowhair children, Linda, seven.

I have seen Bahe Yellowhair come riding in at sundown, herding the sheep into the corral, and his wife Harriet, in her long calico skirt, sitting down in the dirt of the corral, like some mother hen with her chickens. Linda and her brother Bert join their mother. I watch them silently greet all of those who are present, for a Navajo knows each sheep just as an Anglo knows people: one is aggressive, one an agitator; this one is good-natured, another stubborn, another walks with a limp.

Seeing the family among the sheep, and knowing that Harriet Yellowhair is greeting each one, *individually,* I recall the Biblical expression, "The shepherd knoweth his sheep and calleth them by name." In the setting of this isolated hogan, one sees that the Navajo and his sheep share a kinship with nature and comfort one another. It is not too far-fetched to suggest a companionable relationship.

This aspect of their lives reminds me of the altiplano of Peru. The Peruvian Indians also raise sheep, and live in small squalid shelters where they are not much better off, in a physical sense, than the sheep they so devotedly tend. In the altiplano and here in Navajoland, much of the shepherding is done by small children, and trained sheep dogs. But the undertaking is strictly a family affair, and everyone participates.

The sheep's helplessness against predatory animals and their habit of straying absentmindedly from the herd make it essential that the herders maintain constant surveillance, often using sheep dogs. Then the lambing process, when babies are born and must be protected and fed, requires the cooperative efforts of all members of a family. Many of the ewes are what the Navajos call "loco," or crazy, a word borrowed from the Spaniards. When these temperamentally unstable mothers refuse to nurse their lambs, the Navajos must force the mother to accommodate their offspring. Sometimes Harriet Yellowhair has had to prepare canned milk in a baby bottle to feed the lamb herself.

Every member of a family inherits the right to graze livestock within a fairly well-defined area. Land "belongs" to a family such as the Yellowhairs. But the Navajo idea of ownership of such land has been called "inherited use-ownership." The person who "owns" the land controls it for a limited period, and no "owner" can give away or sell land from his family.

Linda, a first-grader and Bessie Yellowhair's youngest sister, already "owns" two lambs with private earmarks. But a Navajo learns from the earliest age that what one "owns" is not for his or her personal benefit but for the benefit of the family. One day a lamb that Linda "owns" will be slaughtered to provide a family meal or contributed to a curing ceremonial when dozens of relatives and friends come to visit and must be fed.

Government charts posted in some trading posts show that it is more profitable to raise beef cattle than sheep, but the Navajos, through some tribal or emotional quirk, appear to have an unshakable attachment to sheep. Possibly the Navajos know better what they can raise profitably than the man in Washington who made the chart. Or, their motives may be psychological. Perhaps they feel that the family who raises sheep together stays together.

Rosemary, now back home with her parents while her husband, a Chippewa, looks for work in Utah, once explained, "Cows are too big. Sheep are just the right size for people." Certainly, watching Linda and Rosemary's five-year-old son George in the corral holding their little lambs, Rosemary's explanation seems eminently logical.

One of the Yellowhair children, Bert, sixteen, is caught

between the sheepherder's world of his father Bahe, and
the white man's world of electric lights, wooden floors, in-
door plumbing and cold soda water. The father has never
been to any school and, typical of about one third of the
Navajos, is illiterate in English, while Bert has been to
Bureau of Indian Affairs schools in Tuba City and Utah,
and so speaks English with reasonable fluency.

On the days that I have lived here in the hogan, I have
studied father and son. Like many sons of "strong" fathers,
Bert has appeared weak, irresolute, irresponsible. I have
gone with him to isolated, lonely, mountainous recesses of
the reservation, and had we come upon a bear or some
other menace, I would have felt better fortified alone than
with Bert as an ally.

On the other hand, Bahe has impressed me as the
epitome of the strength that has permitted the Navajo to
endure. Each morning he leaves with the sheep, each evening he returns. Day in, day out, summer, winter, always,
he and his wife Harriet have shaped their workaday lives
to the grazing needs of their sheep.

Bert falls into a marginal crack, having neither the pa-
tience and hardihood for a sheepherder's existence, nor the
competitive urges required for survival in the Anglo world.
He spends part of his time in school and part on the Tuba
City streets.

On trips to the Keet Seel and Betatakin ruins, inhabited
by the ancient Anasazi people, Bert has sat arrow-straight
on the seat beside me, saying nothing unless I took the
initiative. He has no ideas to volunteer, no idle talk to
exchange; I sometimes forgot he was with me. Returning
from the world of asphalt, high combustion engines, and
soda pop at the trading posts, Bert, who always wears his
"Sunday best," has gone to the corral and sat down in the
dirt, beside his mother, as if he were returning to some

special intimacy served by the sheep, to a sparseness of
life and the mores of a people that shield him from his
inadequacies.

Through my own background in a culture in which
women attempt to mold boys into "men" by making demands upon them, I perceive Bert as infantilized by his
Navajo environment as he invariably returns to his mother,
to lean upon her for comfort, in childlike fashion.

I instinctively find myself crawling through the fenced
logs of entwined piñon and cedar into the corral to share
the family's togetherness. Each of us wants to belong, to
be on the inside with the group, and not, as Santayana
said of white Americans, always paddling your own canoe,
even out on the high seas. It is the togetherness—sitting in
the dirt of the corral with their mother and father and the
sheep—that Linda and Bert will always remember, no
matter what future jobs they hold. A Navajo mother,
Frances Collins, once told me: "We Navajos live much
more intimately than the Anglos."

Earlier this year I went with Frances to visit her husband's parents, Mr. and Mrs. William Collins, Sr., who live
near Iyanbito (meaning Buffalo Springs). Mrs. Leonara
Collins, one of the outstanding Navajo women leaders, is
in her seventies, and her husband is in his eighties. They
continue to be raisers of sheep, although from what little
of the operation I saw during my visit, I could not imagine
that the business was profitable.

Some of the couple's granddaughters, and youngsters
from neighboring hogans, were herding the sheep, but unlike their parents and grandparents who stayed out with
the sheep for days and even weeks and months on end,
these teen-agers were driven to and from the pasture by
pickup truck. And they all carried bottles of soda pop and
bags of Fritos and cookies and looked upon the outing
with the stock more as a lark than as a serious responsi-

bility. They chatted among themselves, in English, about movies they'd seen in Gallup.

Judge Chester Yellowhair of Tuba City, Chief Justice Kirk, former Chief Justice Murray Lincoln and Judge William Leupp all told me that they had led lonely lives as youths, guarding herds of sheep in the wind, sleet, snow; in the summer months, they lived in lean-to brush shelters, to be near the stock.

Judge Leupp recalled, "I used to go with my mother—I was very attached to my mother—and when I was five I told her, 'The sheep you give me, let's don't have their ears cut, it doesn't look good. And we know our sheep, we don't need to brand them.' So my mother quit cutting the sheep's ears from then on.

"Our maximum capacity was two hundred forty sheep. My mother knew every one of them. We had a mix-up of sheep one time with a neighbor, but my mother went out there, and she identified every one of ours. She had seen each one born, helped them nurse. So you get to know them, they become characters, just like people.

"I read in the Bible, 'We are like sheep.' And 'As a sheep before his shearers, he openeth not his mouth.'

"I used to be ashamed to say I was a sheepherder," the judge said. "But now I'm not. I think my education came from herding sheep. I'm glad I had that experience. And maybe I can use it now. A sheep is the most delicate animal. They easily get lost. They're so tender, they can't fight back, they don't even have any teeth. A coyote can take one bite and kill a sheep. People are like that, we have only a short life to live. We're so delicate, we get hurt by the least little thing—and we're done."

Judge Leupp said that in the depression year of 1933, "there were about forty thousand Navajos and they owned over a million sheep, goats and lambs. The land was overgrazed. So the U.S. Government carried out a livestock reduction program. They shot thousands of our sheep, goats and lambs and left them to rot. The Navajos all saw this waste as appalling, incomprehensible. Twenty years later, largely as a result of Government livestock reduction, stock had been reduced by over fifty percent.

"The Navajos always have been frustrated and bitter about the stock reductions," he continued. "They felt the same way you'd feel if I asked you for a fifty-dollar bill, and then after you'd given it to me I burned it up in front of your face."

At a Tribal Council hearing on proposed stock reductions, one old sheep-raiser expressed the Navajo's emotional and economic attachment to his stock:

"Give us our sheep, give us our mutton, let us have herds as our fathers and our grandfathers had. If you take away our sheep, you take away our food, and we have nothing. What then will become of our children? What will they eat and how will they live when they come back to us? You must let us keep our sheep or we die."

Morning: An alarm sounds in the hogan. An alarm? In this eternally peaceful, quiet, enlarged womb—mother earth underneath and around and over me—the strident sound jars my concept of time and place. Perhaps I have died and am buried in some forbidding darkness or entombed with my forebears in a cave. With the clanging alarm, I feel myself suspended between the world of the cave dwellers and the world of atom smashers.

It's six thirty—and Mrs. Yellowhair tells Linda, *time to get up*. She speaks in Navajo, but I can understand. Her voice is my mother's voice. Time to get up and go to school. I am back with my mother and I dress by a warm blazing gas fire. I eat a bowl of piping hot oatmeal with rich milk from our cow, and drink a cup of hot cocoa. I now exist in that unreal reality of a half-forgotten childhood, and this other reality, the hogan, the world that you dream is sweetly innocent until the alarm sounds, until Mrs. Yellowhair turns on the small, battery-operated radio. A rush of transient thoughts assail me: better to lie here, not to be up and about. No way to brush my teeth, anyhow, I don't have a brush, or toothpaste, and in a hogan, there's no water to spare, not a single drop.

Life in the hogan is like life in a small cubicle apartment of Japan, where there are gestures of courtesy, the people living and moving almost as closely as the parts of a watch. We are too crowded in this hogan not to be quiet.

No matter how crowded a hogan may be with its sleeping figures, no Navajo may step over the recumbent body of another. Traditionally, a mother-in-law and son-in-law must never look into each other's eyes. The old taboos seem strangely superstitious until you come to live in such close quarters, and then you begin to see they serve a purpose. Life this close would not work with too many words, too much invasion of another's right to privacy.

I am glad that I'm not expected to get up cheerfully, manufacture meaningless words: good morning, how did you sleep? I slept fine. No one starts "seeing" another until that person wants to be seen. So he or she lives in a "private" world, only a few feet in size.

I lie on the sheepskins listening to a sports announcer tell of a ladies' golf tournament, and my eyes finally focus on Mrs. Yellowhair stoking wood in the old iron stove. She has not been out of Navajoland; what does she know or care about bulletins issuing from a radio, of jet sets' birdies and holes-in-one? I listen to the body count of dead in Vietnam and to details of another hijacked plane. Here the Yellowhairs still travel by horse-drawn wagon.

The night seemed ten nights long. The ground was unyielding and cold. Despite my natural padding on rump and thigh, I still needed to shift positions because the earth's vast rock worked its way into my bones. I tried to remind myself that I was wedged in among people—fourteen of us in this room—that I could not feel lonely, that life was full, that I was not abandoned and empty.

But why this ache in a heart that wrestles with itself, asking questions the head can't know? Why am I on this floor? I already know about sleeping on hard places. Now what can I learn from this earth?

I recall railroad stations in Germany where, shortly after World War II, I stretched out on a bench, bone-weary and grateful to have an opportunity to lie down. And a Chinese fishing junk sailing out of Hong Kong where only the planks of the ancient old vessel served as my bed, the stars my covering for the night. But these were only physical discomforts, and as an adventurer who loves and seeks the picaresque, I have always been able to meet the exigencies of the moment with suitable fortitude.

In their dirty-as-dirt life, the Yellowhairs live on the floor day in, day out. And yet why does she, Harriet Yellowhair, look at me as if she has secrets my heart wants to know?

Get up—Linda, time to go to school, and Mrs. Yellowhair repeats her injunction. I crawl out, like a furtive animal emerging from his mound of earth, certain that the outside world will be hostile. The cold air strikes me hard across the face. On, out into the sand; luckily all the land bends, curves. You don't need a bush, you squat out in the Great Eternity.

When I return I sit on my sheepskins, silent. I watch Linda, who seems small for her seven years, get out from the covers. She does not need to "get dressed." Like the rest of us, she has slept in her clothes. Her mother takes her in her lap, laces her shoes, and re-plaits her hair into two long braids.

Last night I held Linda on my lap, and teasingly asked,

wouldn't she be my little girl? She weighs little more than a doll and has appealing, Mongolian slanted eyes. How, I asked, did she like school? "Oh, I *love* school," she said—animatedly, as an Anglo would. Did she mean her words, or was she attempting to say what she thought was expected of her? Now, she looks at me warily, like a wild animal with its trainer. And yet no one here, not her parents or the others, has been so trusting, so generous in her affections. I did not coax her to my lap; she approached spontaneously, as a cat might do.

Without speaking a word or overtly seeing me, she walks out the hogan door, and I follow just behind her. As we walk through the sand, I make deliberate tracks so that I can find my way back. We are following a path Linda knows instinctively, but all of the earth stretches out to infinity for me. I cannot even discern a road, but Linda finds the ruts that pass for one. After a walk of twenty minutes we stop at a junction, some tracks in the desert of sand, where Linda waits each school morning for a minibus that will deliver her, and other Indian children, to the Red Lake elementary school.

Linda and I have nothing really to say to one another; we are like two people who must stand in silence, yet together, waiting for an elevator. And I don't know why I must be standing out in the freezing cold; it is not I who must go away to school.

Linda, I tell her, I'm cold.

Traditionally a Navajo does not stare into your eyes. But now, she turns dark accusing eyes on me. Without saying a word she is telling me: you came this far, but you will leave, who can trust you?

I leave her, and walk, then run, back up a hill, and look down, and there she stands, kicking one foot into the sand. She looks up to me, and I wave. But she will not wave back. She kicks again, and I see the sand fly.

Then she turns, starts toward me. She does not want to be left alone, going out to *my* world and the Anglo school and the harsh ways of a high-heeled, sharp-voiced Anglo teacher, and see me returning to *her* world, to her mother who takes her in her lap and laces her shoes, and the warm iron stove, and the fry bread. Linda is running toward me, but the mini-bus comes in view and the driver honks the horn for her, and she momentarily pauses—between her two worlds—and slowly turns and gets on the bus.

Linda leaves one world—the hogan, the sheep, a simple, deeply religious life—and goes into another world, that of the *beligaana bit oltaka,* the white man's school. Since it is a day school, she will return to her Indian world at night.

Washington officials say it is part of their enlightened policies to permit Linda to live in two worlds, and thus to retain, to some extent, an identity with her home and parents and religion.

Previously, both church and state have felt Indian parents were a corrupting influence. Since the Federal Government built the first Navajo boarding school in 1883 at Fort Defiance, it has had but one thought in mind for a child such as Linda: bleach her white.

One school superintendent in 1885 opposed day schools because the "barbarian child of barbarian parents" would spend only six of the twenty-four hours of the day in a school, and at the end of each day would "eat and play and sleep after the savage fashion of his race." No, better to "take him away from barbarous life and put him into the enjoyment of civilized life [and] teach him to appreciate, by experiencing them, the comforts of the white man's civilization."

Indian language, a vital emblem of culture, was to be rooted out. The Commissioner of Indian Affairs wrote in his Report of 1886–87, "There is not an Indian pupil whose tuition and maintenance is paid for by the United States Government who is permitted to study any other language than our own vernacular—the language of the greatest, most powerful, and enterprising nationality beneath the sun."

The Navajos were unimpressed by the white man's burden of building great empires. They saw only that their children were dragged from their hogans and taken to harsh prisons where they were maligned and beaten. In 1892 a Navajo named Black Horse attacked a school superintendent for the cruel treatment given Navajo children. A council meeting was called, and one spokesman said, "When we see our children taken from us it is like giving our hearts up."

A father said, "When my boy went to the Fort Defiance school, he had two eyes. The next time I saw him, he had only one." A mother complained, "My son was held prisoner in the belfry of the school, without food. When he was allowed to go to the schoolyard he had handcuffs on his ankles. He escaped, crawling on his hands and knees. When a short distance from home he sank to the ground, exhausted; I found him, and carried him into the hogan."

Indian boarding schools were in effect military establishments. Long Indian hair had to be cut Anglo style. Everyone must dress white, eat white, talk white, think white. It was deemed *un*-American to be Indian; the Navajo must be scourged of that malady, rid of the disease that kept him *different*.

Countless thousands of Indians returned from the *beliganna* schools still red on the outside, but white on the inside—"apples" as the Indians call these misfits. The white man's school did not fit them for the white world, and made them unfit, in many instances, to return to the Indian world of the hogan.

An example of the dislocation was related by Navajo Judge Leupp: "They sent my father, when he was a boy, to Sherman boarding school in California and kept him there for twelve years, and when he came back to the reservation, he had forgotten his own language. He couldn't talk with his own parents, nor they with him."

Another Navajo, Peterson Zah, said that when he was in boarding school "if you spoke Navajo you got your mouth washed out with soap. I never had a white teacher who knew Navajo, yet one called me 'dense' for the crime of not knowing her language."

Zah related that when the late Senator Robert F. Kennedy visited one BIA school, he asked the superintendent, "Do you teach Indian culture and Indian history" And the white superintendent had replied, disdainfully, "These Indians have no history."

Zah also said that "a recent critique of the depiction of the Indian in over three hundred American history textbooks, many of them used by missionary and Bureau of Indian Affairs schools today, illustrates how American children are taught that the Indians were treacherous, decadent, godless and bloodthirsty and that the theft of their lands by white settlers was compatible with the doctrine of 'manifest destiny' and the need to bring Christian civilization to the pagans."

As one example, he said that a Grants, New Mexico, high school textbook, in use in 1972, describes Indians as "savages" who should all be exterminated.

Consumer advocate Ralph Nader, who thinks the Indians should run their own schools, has charged that the white man's schools "breed despondency, cultural inferiority and alienation; it is not surprising that the dropout rate exceeds fifty percent."

The Bureau of Indian Affairs substantiated these charges in its own investigative report, issued in 1972, showing that Indian students in one school had suffered "criminal malpractice" and "physical and mental perversion" by school staff members. "Youngsters reported they were handcuffed for as long as eighteen hours in the dormitory . . . the permanent wrist scars on one youngster's arms, the deformed hand of another boy, and an obviously broken and misshaped rib on another tended to reveal the veracity of student statements."

Studies by the Harvard Center for Law and Education in 1972 revealed that "by every standard, Indians receive the worst education of any children in the country. They attend shabby, overcrowded public schools which lack even basic resources, with many teachers openly disrespectful of Indian heritage and culture."

After leaving Linda to get on the mini-bus, I return to the hogan and find Linda's older sister Rosemary, twenty-eight, preparing for a new day. She has poured in a washpan the equivalent of a cup of water—a rather lavish amount for personal use—and is washing her face and also cleaning the face of her infant Gladys and her son George. When a Navajo uses this much water for a private toilet, it's the equivalent of a Saturday night bath. Where might "we" be going? I am curious but remain silent, having immersed myself into the lives of the Yellowhairs, to go as they go, no questions asked. For the time being, my sense of initiative has been abandoned to this Indian family.

I plunge into the task of washing pots and pans, sweeping "dirt" off the dirt floor. *Hang loose, have no plans, and*

*the plan will work. One must be so flexible that he feels
"lost" and only then will he be saved. But at times it seems
a strain always to remember to let yourself be loose. It's
a strange feeling for the Anglo to hold himself loose.*

As I finish sweeping the debris off the dirt floor, I recall that Rosemary mentioned the possibility of her working as a teacher's aide—caring for the children in one of
the BIA schools—and I assume that's where "we" are
going. Casually I ask if she plans to see about the job,
and she nods affirmatively. It's at Kaibito, a remote community about three hours' drive from here.

When we leave, Rosemary sits up front in the Volkswagen, holding her infant Gladys, and George, five, sits
in back. The children are always so quiet they seem to
have built-in tranquilizers.

After going first to Tuba City to fill up with gasoline—
service stations in the desert can't be taken for granted,
as they are often fifty miles apart—then we drive north,
turning off the pavement onto a rough dirt road for the
trip to Kaibito. Along the way I ask Rosemary: how did
she meet her Chippewa husband?

"At the Inter-mountain school, in Utah," she tells me.

"I was fourteen. And I was there for four years. I went
up there with a girl friend, from across the canyon. She
cried all the time she was up there. She finally gave up
and came back. She was the only person I knew; I was so
lonely. They put me in a retarded or slow group. I just got
so lazy. Everybody just drew, they weren't reading. If
someone tells you that you can't learn you believe it.

"I just lost hope. It's bad to have someone tell you that
you are dumb. And if your teacher tells you, then you
think—she must know, she must be right. When I was
in that class for the retarded, I wanted more than what
they were doing. But the average teacher who was there
couldn't care less what was happening.

"We were not allowed to speak Navajo. If we did, even in the dormitory, we were punished. We were taught that the Navajo religion, the Medicine Man and all of our ways were bad and that we must not be like our parents. Once a teacher got very angry and said, 'If you want to live in a hogan for the rest of your life, just don't bother to learn English!'

"I always talked with my teacher, I'd go up and talk with her, bother her. Just anything to get some attention. One day she came up to me and said, 'Would you like to go to another class?'

"So I went with another group.

"At that time I didn't know which grade I was in. The students were doing some things that were hard work, and I had gotten so lazy that I didn't want to do anything. So this new teacher was always getting after me, spanking me. And she said, 'You don't belong here.' But the other teacher said, 'Just give her a chance. I think they put her in the wrong class to begin with.' Then I caught up. In just four months, I made up what I had lost in a year.

"Some of the students could not bear the regimentation and loneliness of that school," she continues. "One man hung himself while I was there. He was a Navajo, he was from a family that was educated. He had an argument with the housekeeper in the dorm, he wouldn't go to bed, and they tied him up. I didn't see him, but I can just *feel* how they treated him. They put him in jail, and then he tore up his shirt and he hung himself."

When we reach Kaibito, a community consisting of little more than the chapter house and the school complex, we seek out the superintendent, a Mr. Hankins, who sits in his office typing a speech he plans to give to the Gallup Rotarians. He once taught Rosemary in the Red Lake

school, and welcomes us into his office. Rosemary is holding Gladys her baby, and George stands stolidly at her
side. Hankins appears to direct his remarks at me and
keeps referring to "these people" and "they" as if dealing
with aliens.

"They have a long way to go," he says, unconcerned
that "they" are listening. It seems to me to be a deliberate
effort to demean Rosemary and her children, even though
he speaks matter-of-factly, without malice.

"There are 134,000 of these people, and only thirty-eight
teachers among them," he says, with bureaucratic precision.

It was the hackneyed theme, a white man asserting his
sense of cultural superiority, tinged with scorn, over a
non-white: *Can't do this overnight.*

"Now, the young people are a different story," he continues.

Yes, I interpose, trying to be casual and lighthearted.
The Navajos are taking over their own education. And,
one of them might have your job.

Hankins looks disturbed, frowns slightly. "They don't go
in for teaching," he insists. "I asked a Navajo about this,
why more of them didn't become teachers, and the Navajo
studied for a while and then said, 'We hate to tell others
what to do.'"

His story amuses him. When he stops chuckling, Rosemary asks him about a job as teacher's aide and he shuffles
in a drawer and hands her a questionnaire, and assures her
he'll do all he can to help.

He seems typical of the "liberal, good" white who goes
out to help poor Indians and blacks, but who always insists that whites remain in charge, leaving the Rosemarys
of his world the menial tasks of wiping the blackboards
and cleaning up the place.

Rosemary is fully qualified to teach Navajo children.
To meet the *needs* of Navajo children, not some review

board in Washington, Rosemary is, in fact, more qualified than Hankins himself, knowing as she does the thoughts and ways of her people, their language and their capabilities. A good teacher's primary purpose is to motivate his pupils. When an average person remembers the one or two good teachers he's had in his life, it's a fair guess they are those who made him *want* to learn.

Rosemary completes the application and leaves it with Hankins.

We leave Kaibito, and since we will pass through Red Lake about the time that Linda gets out of school, we decide to pick her up.

When we get to the school building, Rosemary's baby Gladys begins to cry for the first time during the trip, and Rosemary stays in the car, while I go into school, with George in hand.

I approach an Anglo teacher who has thin, spindly legs arched on high heels and hair so perfectly groomed it can't be real, and large proud bosoms she displays like a flag. She looks George over, and recognizes him as one of Linda's relatives. I tell her we're here to pick up Linda. "Are you one of Linda's sisters?" she asks. And I see myself in that moment as she sees me—I am dressed like a Navajo, I have long straight hair, parted in the middle, and, to her, I look poor.

Yes, I dissemble, I'm Linda's sister.

"You can wait in the cafeteria," she tells me, and George and I go in and take a bench at the back.

She has not "seen" me at all. I recall an earlier trip with Wilma Veres, a young Navajo mother, taking her children, Debbie, eight, and Bill, seven, back to the Twin Wells Indian School in Holbrook, Arizona. When we went into the Christian mission school, a chapel program was in progress with the children singing, "Onward, Christian Soldiers," in English.

Wilma and her children and I sat at the back and an

Anglo teacher, assuming Wilma and I were sisters, asked me, "Are you Debbie's aunt?" Her question pleased me since I wanted to "pass" for a Navajo. Turning, I smiled broadly, and said, Oh, thank you!

"Oh, maybe you're not a Navajo?" she said, confused. But seeing me dressed as Wilma was dressed—we both had on Navajo skirts and blouses and flat, inexpensive shoes— she added, "But you look Navajo, you have Navajo features."

If these Anglo women are typical, then it won't be any problem for me to "pass" as a Navajo. I have already done so twice without design. My reverie is interrupted when I see that Linda and the other children at Red Lake school are lined up in the hallway. They now march in single file into the cafeteria to be served trays with chocolate milk, a cookie and an apple. They are fed on their arrival in the mornings, and before they leave in the afternoons.

Linda sits at a table that appears high for her, and she and several others rest their arms on the table, but Anglo teachers march up and down the rows of tables like drill sergeants inspecting the troops:

"Linda! Take your arms off the table!"

"Jimmy! Use your napkin!"

Until they came to this school, children such as Linda had never sat down to a table and had never seen napkins.

After the snack, Linda joins us and sits quietly in the back seat with George. Arriving home she does not change her "best" dress but runs to the corral, and sits there, with her mother in her other world.

Two days later: Rosemary and I drive to Tuba City, where I buy canned goods, sugar, flour, coffee and a big sack of potatoes. We stop at the Red Lake school on the way home, and I go in and say I'm there to get Linda.

The Anglo teacher, still assuming I'm Linda's sister, tells me: "Her *other* sister already got her."

I'm confused, but don't ask any questions, and back at the car, I repeat to Rosemary what the teacher has said.

"Oh, it must be Mary," Rosemary says immediately, adding, "I guess she's come in from Phoenix."

I have heard the names of Rosemary's twelve brothers and sisters, but have trouble keeping them sorted out, remembering their whereabouts and what they do. Mary lives in Phoenix—and picks oranges? I ask Rosemary, testing my memory. And Rosemary nods. And she's younger? I ask.

"Yes, nineteen," Rosemary says, adding that in the last letter Mary mentioned a friend with whom she picks oranges, an Anglo named Connie who has a car, and that they plan to drive to the hogan.

When we return to the hogan, a sedan is parked outside. It's a decrepit vehicle that has seen better days.

When we go in, I learn the sedan belongs to the Anglo, Connie, who has driven here with Mary Yellowhair.

Mary is a well-proportioned and attractive woman with short or bobbed hair. Mary has brought her boyfriend, an Indian named Jimmie. The Anglo, Connie, seems to displace half the area of the hogan. She's a huge, hippo-shaped woman, twice the width of Mrs. Yellowhair. She's obviously a stranger to the hogan. "You mean your family doesn't even have a toilet? Not a toilet of *any kind*?" she asks Mary incredulously, not once but several times. Connie has dirty-blond streaked hair that hangs like dry, stiff straw around her face. She appears unkempt, unattended and a bit waifish.

The weather has been blustery, and the family and I are going through our ritual of getting rid of the day, shutting out the outside noise and confusion and simply living within ourselves for a while. Even in the midst of people, we are accustomed to quiet, but Connie's presence is disturbing. She twists and turns her body, constantly moving her arms and hands and speaking animatedly, compulsively, as though she will be punished if she stands mute.

"It sure is quiet in here!" she punctuates her monologue, and Mary, resting on sheepskins with Jimmie, murmurs a soft "*ohhh*," an all-purpose Navajo word that means yes.

"I don't see how you stand it," Connie continues, now talking more to herself than to the rest of us. She's like so much gaseous matter under pressure, and one senses that if she doesn't escape the confines of these mud-plastered walls she will explode from some inner tension. It isn't just one thing about the hogan that bothers her. It is the total nothingness.

Mrs. Yellowhair makes no move to begin an evening meal. All I can see in sight for supper are the potatoes. Mr. and Mrs. Yellowhair, Rosemary and her children and Linda get ready for bed, and I go out under a magnificent canopy of stars and cloudlessness. As I walk through the sand, wanting, perhaps, to clear my mind of Connie's magnified chatter, I feel I have lost all sense of direction. I can no longer see the hogan. In the dark vastness, I am reduced to another grain of sand.

When I return, Mary and Connie are eating some of the potatoes, which Rosemary has boiled, and I eagerly join them. We stand around the cupboard, putting on generous gobs of free butter which the U.S. Department of Agriculture distributes in large tin cans as part of its "dole" to its Indian wards. Along with huge chunks of butter, we sprinkle salt and pepper and hot red pepper sauce to make a surprisingly piquant dish of a commonplace staple.

"Butter! Real butter. I've never tasted butter," Connie says, maintaining her nonstop chatter.

Why, I ask, hadn't she ever tasted butter?

"I come from a margarine family," she says.

Without any encouragement, Connie babbles on, revealing that her mother once was a model, that her mother and her new stepfather live in Los Angeles, and that she, Connie, "dropped out" of school and moved to Phoenix two years ago. She looks "hippie," but clearly is unprepared for the simple life.

The Navajos arrange the sheepskin bedding on the hogan's dirt floor to accommodate family and guests. Each knows his or her territory for the night. I am sandwiched between the young lovers, Mary and Jimmie, and Mr. and Mrs. Yellowhair.

The next morning, Connie collects her few personal items, such as purse and sweater, preparing to leave this sparse environment for the creature comforts of her own pad. "I don't mind the lack of water so much," she whispers to me, "but there's not even an outhouse!"

Mary and her boyfriend Jimmie, acclimated to the bright lights and sounds of Phoenix, decide to go with Connie. Preparing to leave, Mary uses the common washbowl, splashing water on her attractive face. As completely guileless as if she were in a private dressing room, she pulls off a sweater, and her perfect pomegranate breasts are encased in a white uplift brassiere. From her exposed flesh, naked to the waist except for the bra, my eyes travel to the face of her father, who apparently sees only the cup of coffee he has in hand.

Mary's action surprises me because I have never seen anyone else in the hogan dressing or undressing. Rosemary, when she has changed her clothes, has adroitly held a blanket around her. The discretion and modesty that have prevailed are casually violated by this daughter from the city.

I decide to drive to Navajo Mountain, one of the most isolated regions in the United States, and visit the small boarding school there. Bert Yellowhair goes along with me, and we drive fifty-five miles over a winding, rocky mountainous road. I look out on the sand blasts of ages, a disorderly, unsymmetrical rock jumble that dissolves into well-ordered cliffs, one thousand feet high, so straight one thinks they might have been carved by knife.

I pick up two hitchhikers, an old typically dressed Indian couple en route to the Inscription House trading post. I ask Bert to sit in back with her, and the old man, who is badly crippled, sits up front with me, practicing the English he learned years ago working for the railroad off the reservation. The old woman talks constantly with Bert in Navajo, and later he tells me she said she and Bert belonged to the same clan but that he had never heard of her.

Halfway to our destination, the old couple get off at the trading post and Bert and I continue north. At the end of the road we find the oasis, a small settlement composed of a one-room school, a building where the children sleep and eat, and a few small homes, one belonging to Councilman Harold Drake and his family, another to the schoolteacher, Miss Blanche Barrows.

When we walk into the one-room school, Miss Barrows, a large black woman from Texas with an expansive personality, stops her instructions, nods a greeting to me, and immediately says to Bert, "You're a Yellowhair, aren't you? I taught your sister in Red Lake." I learn she has never before seen Bert, but recognizes him as a Yellowhair because he has the same facial characteristics as a sister who was in her classroom eight years ago.

Miss Barrows presents us to her class, and we take two of the children's miniature chairs and listen while the class continues. The teacher keeps them on their feet by allowing any child with an answer to come up front and address the group with his or her observations. I learn that Miss Barrows has recently borrowed a big school bus and, driving it herself, has taken the entire class on a trip to Disneyland in California.

"Tell our visitors about what you saw," she suggests.

I expect to hear about Mickey Mouse, but instead one small Indian says he stayed in a motel and it had television, and a young girl is telling about her experience of riding in an elevator.

Certainly the children were seeing such man-made wonders as motels and television and elevators for the first time. But I am not prepared to deal with these impressions. They seem too trite, maybe even rehearsed. On the other hand, should you bring a ghetto child to the reservation, what might impress him? He's grown up with television and elevators, but he would be impressed by what every Indian child takes for granted, just plain space.

After the classwork is over, Miss Barrows invites us for milk and cookies in the small cafeteria. She arranges for Bert and me to spend the night, Bert to stay in the building with the students, and I in Miss Barrows' home, which is next door to the little schoolroom. In the evening, as we talk, she tells me of coming to this isolated area:

"After I got past Kayenta and left the pavement and came to all the jagged upturned rocks, and no people, I thought I'd come to the end of the world. The only reason I kept going was that I *had* to see what was at the end of this road." At the end of the road, she found the cluster of native stone structures that had been built in 1932 when the school was founded. She was accustomed to rural living in Texas, but nothing to compare with the isolation one experiences at the base of the Navajo Mountain that towers more than 10,000 feet above us.

As a black keenly aware of being perceived as "different" all of her life, Miss Barrows has a special empathy for the Indian children coming to a federally funded school to learn a new life.

"I suppose," she reflects, as we sit in her small kitchen, "it would be like sending a white child to an Indian reservation, and having the child live in a hogan and become a student of a Medicine Man, who would tell him that the faith of his parents, their teachings, their religion, their language, all of these were bad, and that henceforth he must speak only Navajo. The child would go back to his white world every so often, and he would see the difference—but which way would he go? Who would be right? You hear a lot about the pros and cons of the boarding school. But in this kind of isolation, what alternative is there? Around here, the families are too widely scattered to have classrooms close to the hogans. And the parents want the schools. They know they can't give the child what the schools provide. There are more and more Navajos and less and less grazing lands. So the children must be trained, must have other ways to make a living, besides raising sheep."

Blanche Barrows' spotlessly clean house with its big, high bed and fluffy counterpane and the good smells in the kitchen reminds me of a reunion at home at Christmas time. I feel "sister" with her: we have the same myths, the same Jesus Christ, God the Holy Father, the Holy Spirit, Three Gods in One; the same ideals and goals. And for us, though we are loath to admit it, these Indians are "them," *the different ones.*

Blanche and I sit down to our evening meal with a Navajo woman who works as her assistant, a teacher's aide, the same kind of job that Rosemary wants. Her name is Elsie, and she has a youthful, unlined face, belying her thirty-two years. While Blanche is dishing up some Southern specialities, I ask Elsie: had she ever seen a black person before she met Miss Barrows?

"No," she tells me. And then she relates how excited she had been as a child when a white man came to their hogan door and asked for water. Elsie did not call him a white man, but rather "a bearded man." Indians do not grow hair on their faces to the extent that white and black Americans do, and when they have soft fuzz, they have traditionally plucked it out—hair by hair. Old Navajo razors were tweezers made from two pieces of shell. The more modern razors are tweezers made from any piece of metal.

As we talk, Blanche loads the table with homemade biscuits and cheesecake, vegetables, fried chicken and pork chops. I have a hunger for down home "soul" cooking that whites and blacks traditionally have eaten in the South, and I greedily reach out and fork myself a pork chop. Blanche helps herself, and Elsie just sits there, staring at us as though we are heathens.

"I don't see how you can eat *pig*," she says.

"Well, I don't see how you can eat sheep," Blanche responds, indicating she maintains an easy camaraderie with her aide. "How can you eat those *humble* little creatures that you raise like pets? You give them milk out of a baby bottle, you name them."

What does Elsie have against pork? I ask.

"Pigs eat anything. They are not clean," she replies.

Blanche and I have decided to eat our fill, Elsie's distaste notwithstanding. After the first course of pork chops, we help ourselves to the fried chicken.

Blanche says, "You know, I've never known a Navajo family to raise chickens on the reservations. It puzzles me because most families could profitably keep a few hens around."

Looking at Elsie's plate we see she's eaten only potatoes and bread. Wasn't she going to taste the chicken? Again she indicates we've offered her an inedible, nauseating dish. But what does she have against chickens?

"Chickens eat worms."

Well, what animals are clean?

"The sheep are sweet and clean. They just eat grass."

"But what about cows?" Blanche asks.

"That's too much meat at one time," Elsie says.

"I know you don't have refrigeration," Blanche reasons. "But you could dry it, make jerky."

But Elsie says, "No, a Navajo likes fresh meat," and she amends that to say, "fresh *mutton*."

Rosemary and I again drive to Kaibito, to talk about her job possibilities. We take her son George.

Returning, we make a detour to visit her grandmother and great-grandmother.

Now I know five generations of Yellowhairs: George and his mother Rosemary, and her father Bahe, who is fifty-five, and *his* mother Rose, who is seventy-five, and Bahe's grandmother Frances, who is one hundred.

Bahe's mother and grandmother are both converts to Christianity, and they live in a small frame house, not much larger than a hogan, but "modern" in that it has a wooden floor and frame beds. There is no toilet—indoors or out.

We are four women, sitting on the sides of two frame beds, and George, five, is the only male among us.

The old grandmother, carved of granite, white-haired, toothless and impish by nature, turns to me.

"Do you know how you can tell intelligence in a woman?" She speaks in Navajo and Rosemary translates, but before I understand the words I know she is teasing me.

All is quiet. Rosemary and Bahe's mother Rose listen attentively, as the aged must always be respected. Otherwise they can "bewitch" you even if they are Christian converts.

"It is known that those women who are small above the

waist but ample below the waist are 'highly intelligent,' "
the one-hundred-year-old woman says, elaborating on the
girth of the hips and backside as signs of intelligence.
"What about you, Grace?" she asks. I have to stand and
show my backside to offer "proof" of my intelligence.

The old woman laughs raucously, and I try to join in.
Her humor reminds me of how as a child my father would
inflate then deflate my ego.

"You know that child has lots of brains," he would tell
people in my presence; then, seeing me swell with pride,
he would add, "but they're all in her heels."

The old grandmother decides to take advantage of the
car outside and asks that we drive her to the trading post.
Bahe's mother Rose, who looks twenty years younger than
her seventy-five, climbs in the back with Rosemary, and I
am helping the one-hundred-year-old-woman up front. She
walks easily enough but has trouble stepping into the
Volks. She jokes:

"Somebody back there is holding onto me. *Let go!* So I
can climb into this car!"

November 1, 1972

I will visit Bessie Yellowhair at her sister's place near Ganado. Early in the morning, I drive across the sand dunes to the paved highway that leads to Tuba City. I drive for two hours on a lonely ribbon of road. I continue past the Steamboat trading post, to a small house made of concrete blocks that stands by the side of the road. I pull up to the house, go to the door and find Bessie alone. She's been ironing and sewing, and she welcomes me with a barrage of Anglo-like complaints:

"Just look at this house. What a mess! I have spent the entire morning cleaning this bathroom," and she shows me a room the size of a telephone booth, with paint peeling off the walls. "And this kitchen, just look at these filthy curtains!" She points to old ones she has taken down and to new ones she's put up. "I got the material for just fifty cents," she says. She has put them up ingeniously with a few hooks, and they add a bright, clean look to the kitchen.

Yes, Bessie is my type of woman. She knows how to *better* herself. I am as comfortable with Bessie as I am with myself; but in many ways her sister Lucy interests me more because she, unlike Bessie, does not attempt to "better" herself, in Anglo fashion. I ask about Lucy.

"She went to a Sing," Bessie tells me.

I can sense Bessie's ambivalence. When she talks she relives, but only briefly, the excitement a Sing must have meant for her as a child. Now she says, "Lucy's always going to Sings. And dragging her children with her." Bessie's tone is "white," and her judgment also: "She should be home cleaning this house!" Bessie, like so many Anglos, is convinced of the work ethic: work-hard-and-you-succeed; and also the soap ethic: cleanliness-is-next-to-godliness.

Simply because we lack anything else to do, Bessie suggests we drive over to the Sing, and perhaps find Lucy. I would like to relax, sit quietly, and talk. But Navajos are increasingly on the go. Many such as Bessie remind me of the New Mexico state bird, called the Road Runner. Now Bessie, Anglo fashion, can't sit still.

We walk to my "bug," but Bessie hesitates.

"Do you have a heater?" she asks.

No, I said. The Volks didn't.

"Oh, you've *got* to have it out here!" Bessie insists.

As we walk to her pickup truck, I reflect on the irony of her "white" convictions.

Then, as we leave the highway and bounce through a gully and then across sand dunes, following tracks that lead off like veins in your skin, Bessie excitedly tells me, "When the Medicine Man at this Sing prays for rain, it always rains." A moment later she berates the rituals. "Once they were sacred and had meaning but now they're just social events and don't mean anything."

Always in her tone and statements I observe her as the marginal Indian woman caught between the world of Medicine Men and air conditioning. She does not nullify her traditions, knowing they are an integral part of life. But she has gained the capacity to see them with a modern detachment.

Just as Bessie might once have believed in a Medicine Man who can pray for rain—"and it always rains"—I once believed in the evangelist who came to our town, and put up a tent and saved men's souls. That was the only "event" for months in our small community. But now Bessie and I have seen televised trips to the moon, and we—more than our parents—turn out to the world and its sensory pleasures, rather than inward, to meditation, mysticism.

Eventually we reach a small frame house, and park alongside other pickup trucks. Bessie tells me that the family and clan will go inside the frame house for a big meal, and then into an adjacent hogan for the Sing. We are enveloped in a blinding dust storm, and Bessie keeps the motor of the pickup running so that we are sealed off from the dust, in warm comfort. Bessie, I know, does not intend to leave this oasis for the dirt and misery of the hogan.

Rather than the ceremonial, Bessie's thoughts turn to Calvin, her boyfriend. "Calvin was coming over today, on his motorcycle," she says. She obviously is impressed by his having a motorcycle.

Sensing she wishes to discuss him further, I ask rather absentmindedly: What's his clan?

"Calvin doesn't know," she says.

But why doesn't he know? I ask. Among Navajos that is equivalent to not knowing your family name.

"When his mother was converted to Christianity, they taught her that having a clan and going to a Medicine Man were evil, and she taught Calvin this way. He doesn't know anything about his religion, or our ways, but sometimes he has bad dreams and he asks me: 'Do you suppose a witch is bothering me?'

"When he asks the question about witches, he doesn't want me to answer and tell him, 'Yes, that's your problem.' Because he's been trained to think logically, and he can't possibly accept the idea of witches."

But can Bessie accept witches?

"Yes, I believe in those things," she replies, candidly, easily.

We sit outside a curing Sing in which we are not really

interested. Shouldn't we return to the house? I ask. "No hurry. If Calvin comes and I'm not there, he'll come back," she says.

Hesitantly, I ask if she and Calvin have sex relations.

"Yes, we have. For three years now," she tells me as casually as she'd relate what she had for lunch.

Does she have any guilt feelings about sex outside of marriage?

"No, and I don't believe the Navajos have that kind of guilt feeling. Sex itself is not forbidden. But you're not supposed to have sex with anyone in your mother's or your father's clan. You're not ever to *touch* these people. When I went to boarding school, the Anglo teacher tried to get some of us to dance, and she put me with one of my clan 'brothers' and she never understood why we just stood there and wouldn't dance."

I remark Western men often "fall in love" with beautiful legs that symbolize sex. Does Bessie think that Calvin sees her that way?

"No, it's different. Indian men don't have the habit of liking to look at pictures of nude women, for example. Once in my office an Anglo was studying *Playboy*—he had it open to one of those centerfolds of a nude woman—and when Calvin came in, the Anglo said to him, 'Just look at this.' And later Calvin said to me, 'Why would he want to look at those pictures?' Calvin says that's the same as a man saying he is hungry and then preferring to stare at food, or say, photos of food, rather than sit down and eat."

I ask Bessie if she and Calvin did anything to prevent her getting pregnant. Did she use birth control pills?

"No, I don't believe in that. I want to be natural. I don't know why I haven't gotten pregnant, but I have never done anything to prevent it."

Many unwed white girls have acted natural, too, but

once pregnant they've had second thoughts and have undergone abortions. Would Bessie ever consider doing that?

"No," she says emphatically. "I would never do that."

Bessie seems to welcome the future, without worry or fear, indicating that to fret about it, analyze it or attempt to shape it is to mistrust the Holy People who make all the big decisions anyway. She relates one story of the Navajos' Holy People, and their acceptance of children born out of wedlock:

"Two youths were questioning their mothers, 'Who are our fathers?' And the mothers said, 'You have no fathers. You are *Yutaski* [illegitimate].' But the boys kept asking, 'Who are our fathers?' and the mothers said, 'The round cactus and the sitting cactus are your fathers.'

"Navajos think it strange when Anglos show us pictures of two white male gods, the Father and the Son," Bessie says. "In our religion we have many women deities. Changing Woman gave corn to the people and she, along with the Sun and the Hero Twins, is one of our main gods. She is the only one who is always good to us. Then we have Salt Woman, who gave us salt, and Spider Woman, who taught us how to weave."

Bessie's stories imply that Navajo women have always been "liberated." Unlike my mythology that teaches me a woman came from a man's rib, the Navajo mythology has placed woman, from the very beginning, as fully equal to man.

And when Bessie talks, it is with self-assurance, with the conviction that she is any man's equal. I find it difficult to imagine the man who might "win" her.

Does she want to marry Calvin? I ask.

"No, I'm not ready to get married," she says. I have no clue whether she is being typically Navajo or a typical average young person today.

"I want to go back to school," Bessie continues. "And Calvin says if I want to stop work, he will help me."

I suggest that Calvin is being generous.

"He will do this," she says, "only if I promise to marry him."

Calvin's stipulation surprises me; it makes him sound so Anglo.

But how was Calvin to prove himself "stronger" than Bessie except by making demands on her? Except by doing it in the conventional way, being the breadwinner? But I learn that Bessie has told Calvin she doesn't think she will require his help, that she feels she can get a scholarship when and if she decides to go away to school.

She's making it difficult for Calvin, I tell her, by being such a "strong," even dominant personality.

"Yes," she agrees, not hesitating a moment to admit her strength. "Navajo women *are* strong.

"In your society, you take your father's name, but we always take the name of our mother's clan. If you get pregnant and are not married, you worry about your child not having a name—you might worry so much you kill the child, but if I am pregnant my child will have my clan name, whether I'm married or not.

"And then Navajo women have always been owners of property. I got my first sheep when I was five years old. I have always had my bit of grazing land," Bessie continues.

"And traditionally the man goes to live with his wife's people. If the couple don't get along, then it is the man who must leave, and the woman keeps everything: the house, the sheep, the blankets. Also, a Navajo woman can always earn money by weaving a rug. The woman, not the man, always has this handy source of income."

Bessie and I are engrossed in our own talk, and only occasionally look out the windows of the pickup truck, at the scene around us. Old fat women stand around open fires, stirring huge pots filled with mutton stew, and others are slapping dough for fry bread. Bessie and I gaze through the window but we are like two persons, deep in a conversation, who look at a moving TV screen that has no sound, that holds our eyes, but not our attention.

"Oh, there's Lucy," Bessie calls out, and her sister, seeing the pickup truck, walks over to where we are parked. As she gets inside, it starts to rain, and Bessie laughs over the Medicine Man's powers, and Lucy scolds her for not being more serious.

"Aren't you staying for the Sing?" Lucy asks.

"No, I've got to get back. I'm expecting Calvin," Bessie says. Lucy says nothing, and leaves us to go with the others into the hogan where the curing ceremonial will now be conducted.

The Sing has meant little to Bessie other than a place to go. Sitting among the other pickup trucks and the moving figures seems more interesting for her than sitting in Lucy's small concrete block house. Eventually we start back.

In the small house, waiting for Calvin, I ask Bessie: isn't she very much impressed by Calvin's owning a motorcycle?

"Yes," she agrees at once. "I like it. We have fun. One weekend we went to Gallup, and another weekend we went to Albuquerque. We go anywhere, and stop anywhere we like along the way."

As we sit discussing Calvin, we hear the roar of the motorcycle and suddenly I see a sturdy, muscular figure standing at the door.

Soon after Calvin comes in, Lucy arrives back home with her three children, ranging from five to ten years. She stays busy with the demands of her children, and Bessie goes into the kitchen to rewarm some fry bread.

When we sit around a kitchen table eating fry bread, which we sprinkle with chili sauce, Calvin looks upon me as some traitor in their midst. I expect a catechism to begin at any moment.

"Bessie tells me you're a *writer*," he begins accusingly, making the word sound like "spy" or "suspect character."

I nod in agreement.

And then the barrage: "What makes you think you have the right to come here and study us? You can't write about our lives, you can't know me. I get sick and tired of people like you coming out to the reservation for a week and then turning out a book, all about Indians."

I listen silently, and Bessie, sitting between us, looks first to him and then to me, as if Calvin is forcing her to take sides.

I like his questioning my motives, I tell Calvin. I always question them myself.

"You can't 'be' an Indian," he insists.

And then we continue the argument, with my telling him that he is right: I can't know *him*. I add that I don't really know myself, much less another.

Should Calvin travel to Japan or Peru he might write home about what he ate, whom he met, what he saw. And I add he has a right to *his* impressions of a place and a people, just as I have a right to mine.

Knowing that he and Bessie would prefer to be alone a part of the evening, I later excuse myself and go to one of the two bedrooms, and crawl into the bed—getting far over to the wall side, presuming that several other persons may eventually be there with me—and go to sleep. In the night I learn I'm sleeping with Lucy and all three of her children.

The next morning, when we are alone, Bessie confides, "Calvin says you're 'using' me."

Yes, that's right, I agree. Friends do "use" one another,

though we shouldn't "misuse" one another. Isn't Calvin using her? Isn't she using Calvin?

Bessie seems to have "found" herself already, to have taken a hold on her identity. Navajo women, like Bessie, are adaptable. Though she believes in witches and never goes to beauty parlors or wears makeup, she is tuned in to Anglo styles and thought patterns. A woman can conform without loss of "identity," but a man must constantly prove his masculinity or be branded a "failure."

I think of Calvin's forebears of three hundred years ago. The Indian man hunted and felt the thrill and excitement of the hunt, and the satisfactions of learning the necessary skills to survive. Compared with the virility of life in the past, the present existence is pallid and soft.

Calvin, with no deep roots in his Indian culture, clings to his Indian-ness more desperately than does Bessie, whose early religious training reinforced her faith in herself as a Navajo woman.

I now plan to get a job and "pass" as a Navajo.

On my brief visit to the reservation in 1969, my brother Ed urged me to go as an "Indian" among the whites.

But what, I had asked, would that prove? I felt that blacks suffered the worst discrimination of any group in this country. And that I had learned in my *Soul Sister* experience as much about whites' injustice to "inferior" people—those with darker pigmentation than our own— as my conscience and grievance capacity could bear.

I told Ed: Indians don't suffer the same degree of prejudice as blacks.

"Are you sure?" Ed had asked.

I argued that the black is encapsulated in his blackness. The white who wants to practice racism has an easy target. But the Indian can "pass," he can leave the reservation any day he wants to.

"He can leave physically, but can he psychologically?" Ed asked. "Don't forget that the Indian and his land are inseparable. If he leaves his land, he leaves his Indian-ness. Whatever he is, whatever he believes, stems from the soil. His country is part of his religion.

"The Indian-American has never been separated from his land," Ed went on. "All the rest of us are fairly recent immigrants—coming of our own free will, or, in the case of the blacks, brought here in chains. The Indian's traditions stem back to a prehistoric past. He has clung to the soil, preferring to die rather than adapt or be assimilated.

"We feared and hated blacks because they're black, and

we didn't want them to be like us; and hated Indians
because they could so easily join the big American melting
pot—but they refuse to melt.

"Now the Navajos have increased in population to the
extent that their soil, already overgrazed and depleted,
will no longer support them. And many are forced to leave
their land and work in big cities."

We had been sitting that day, back in 1969, in his home
in Window Rock, and Ed opened a copy of the Navajo
Times, a weekly newspaper published by the tribe. "Look
at these ads placed by white families wanting to employ
a Navajo girl as a live-in domestic," he said. "The families
will pay your bus fare to New York, Las Vegas, Los Angeles. You can learn why white people a thousand or more
miles from Navajoland want to hire a Navajo."

Then he read one of the ads:

"WANTED: Doctor needs live-in maid to do house-
keeping and care for three small children. One hundred
dollars per month. Prepaid bus ticket to Los Angeles."

But a doctor makes good money, I responded. Why
would he bring someone from an Indian reservation? Why
can't he hire someone in Los Angeles?

"This doctor will pay a Navajo only a hundred dollars
a month. Do you know any white or black woman who
would work for twenty-five dollars a week, washing, ironing, scrubbing, and taking care of several small children?"
Ed asked.

I suggested that a poverty-stricken *latina* newly arrived
from south of the border might take the job.

"Then there are other reasons why the doctor prefers the
Navajo. Almost any single girl uses the phone, goes to
movies, watches television and goes on dates at night. The
average Navajo girl has no phone or electricity in the
hogan, she's not accustomed to television or the movies,

and she doesn't go out at night. She will simply stay home and work."

Doing all the housework and taking care of several young children sounded like a ten- or twelve-hour-a-day job. And what, I asked, about minimum wage?

"They get around the law somehow by giving you room and board," Ed said. "White and black Americans are competitive enough to know that it's better to work by the hour. But the Indian, who has never been money-minded or as competitive as the rest of the society, remains very vulnerable."

Now I learn that Bessie Yellowhair once responded to one of the ads in the Navajo *Times* for live-in domestic help, and that she went to work for a white family in Santa Barbara, California.

I can hardly contain my curiosity about Bessie's adventures as a maid, and when we are alone, I ask her to tell me all about them.

> It was in 1960. A priest told me about this job. The woman who hired me arranged for me to pick up a prepaid ticket at the bus station. And the priest drove me to Holbrook. I was fourteen. I remember I was crying when I got on the bus at Holbrook. And I felt so lost when I got to Los Angeles, so many people, I didn't know which gate to go to, I didn't know where to go, and whether I was supposed to stay there or get on another bus to go to Santa Barbara. I wasn't sure what to ask, which bus to get on. Because I wasn't so sure of my language. So I slept up there on one of those hard benches in the women's rest room. I cried that night because I didn't know where I was. The next morning, I asked one lady if she could help me, but she just got up and left. Finally

I found this other lady who was working there, and she helped me; she said you're supposed to go here, and get on the bus, and she tried helping me find my suitcase—I had lost it when I changed buses. When I got to Santa Barbara and got off the bus I didn't have anything, just my jacket with me, and that was it.

This white lady who had put the ad in the paper met me but I really felt lonely. And lost. When we got to the place where the family lived, she took me to a laundry room. Then she said, "This will be your room." I saw these stacks of sheets and towels, and dirty clothes in a basket, and I thought maybe she's putting me here just temporarily, but she never moved me. I hardly talked. I talked with the smallest boy, but he wasn't old enough to talk back. He was the one I had to stay with all the time, the other two were school age. Everyone was always gone, or on the go. When the boys got up they just disappeared, and when they were at home they didn't hardly talk. When one of the little boys would speak up, the father would reprimand him—"Wait, I'm talking"—in a really harsh voice. And I was afraid to say anything, afraid he'd say, "Shut up! I'm talking."

And when I'd be cleaning house, there'd always be machines that are noisy, vacuum sweepers, and outside there'd be cars and horns and sirens. It was like being in jail, I'd look out those windows. I was scared. My head felt like it was spinning with all that noise around me. Twenty-four hours a day noises were going. It was never like home. At home you wake up in the morning and the first thing you hear are birds singing. At home I could go outside and know that over the hills there would be just space. But at that house, if I looked out, there'd be another building sitting there.

They weren't interested in me, my religion, what kind of life I led as Indian, or my background. No, they just wanted me to work. And keep working like a machine. The house was so big, too lonely. I wouldn't want to live in a place like that. No one loved the others, the parents never touched the children. The smallest boy was sick, and the mother was out partying. I sat there with the little boy, and felt sorry for him.

I didn't even think about getting away, because I knew I had to stay there. I didn't know which way to go or where to go to, to get away. I didn't know any people. I knew that it took me many hours on a bus to get there, and that it was so far away that I couldn't get back. Not until I had worked a year, the time I was supposed to be there.

The work got worse. At first she wasn't so bad, but then she just got to piling work on me, like the ironing. I had ironed all day and part of the evening and when I got through with the shirts, she brought them all back, and said, "Do them over." I cried when she brought back all those shirts. I thought about my mother. I had to ask myself, why did I leave home, to do this kind of thing? I was never treated like that, I was always free at home. For breakfast I was only getting fruit, maybe half an apple or half a grapefruit, half a banana, that was it, and I was working on my feet all day with maybe just a little sandwich for lunch. Sometimes the lady would plan for a party. And maybe that evening I'd eat a sandwich and go upstairs with the kids to put them to bed.

I was really hungry one evening, so I went down to where they store their food, and got a can of beans. I took it up to my room, but I didn't know how to open it. I didn't bring up an opener or anything, so

I couldn't eat it. So I left it under the bed, and I never took it back down. I'd still be hungry in the mornings. She'd say, "I'm leaving to visit a friend, so just do this and that, just keep working . . ." So as soon as she'd leave maybe I'd get a cracker and run to my room and eat it, as fast as I could before anybody could see me.

I was supposed to be making twenty-five dollars every two weeks; the lady told me that she was sending it to my mother. I wasn't worried about getting it into my hands, but I was worried about maybe she wasn't getting it to my mother. And I'm not sure whether she ever did send the money, because my mother never said anything about getting the money. Up to this day my mother and I have never discussed the money that I earned, because that wasn't the important thing; the only important thing was that I got back. She didn't ask me how much money I made. The woman never gave me any money. I never bought any clothes, anything. I remember I used a paper bag to bring my things back.

Bessie and I drive from Lucy's house back to the Yellowhair hogan. Inside the hogan, Bessie and I take dippers of water from a community pail, and even while we are drinking I notice the mother, Harriet Yellowhair, has begun to make fry bread. It is almost supper time, but this is her gesture of welcome.

Traditionally the Navajos have lived in isolation, often herding sheep for days on end; and whenever two or more come together, it is an occasion for celebration, for food—if there is food on hand.

"I haven't seen my mother for a week," Bessie reminds

me, speaking in a tone an Anglo might use to say she hasn't seen her mother in a year.

The Anglo might write his mother, or telephone, or send a check. But the Navajo will go in person. It is this need for the presence of the loved one that preserves the intimacy, the unity, of the Navajo family.

On the drive here, I have confided to Bessie my plan to answer one of the want ads in the Navajo *Times*, and to work for a white family in California. After the mother has served Bessie and me fluffy morsels of hot fry bread, sprinkled liberally with salt, she sits beside us, on the floor; and Bessie tells her mother in Navajo my plan to go to work as a live-in domestic, just as Bessie did some years ago.

An expression of sorrow clouds the mother's face. The memory obviously remains painful. The mother tells me, with Bessie as interpreter, "But you will be so *alone*."

It is my aloneness that most intrigues and baffles the Navajo. The "poor" man or woman to the Navajo is the one who acts as if he doesn't have a single relative. Now she sees me as she saw her own daughter, leaving the circle of those who will provide for you and going, alone, into the cruel world where greed for possessions separates brother from brother, child from mother.

Bessie begins to plan my wardrobe. "You won't need much. Remember, a Navajo girl who took that kind of job wouldn't have many clothes, she'd just be carrying a small bag." And then, laughing: "Maybe you won't lose your suitcase like I did."

Taking off her most prized silver-and-turquoise bracelet, she reminds me, "Even the poorest Navajo wears jewelry. Take this." When I protest, she shames me, "You are like a sister."

I put the Bessie Yellowhair bracelet on my arm and I

rub the beautiful large stone. It is the greenish hue that Navajos call the female stone—the clear, deep robin's-egg-blue turquoise they call male. Already, I feel less lonely.

Bessie finds an old, inexpensive canvas suitcase, with a flowered design. "This is exactly right," she tells me. Then she chooses an old, well-worn long cotton gown. "You don't have to be so traditional that you sleep in your clothes," she laughs.

She suggests that I wear tennis shoes, white socks. And a long skirt with blouse. Bessie offers me one of her skirts and blouses, and I readily accept.

The skirt is large in the waist; I stand while the mother fits it to my figure, and then we sit together while she sews up the seams. "These are old, but they are just right," Bessie assures me.

The next morning, I leave the family and return to Window Rock. I check into a motel room and make plans for applying for the job.

I study the Navajo *Times* with a growing apprehension, anxious to make the right choice.

> *Wish to hire* a live-in domestic. To care for four-year-old boy. Starting salary $100.00 a month. With room and board. (With an address in Thousand Oaks, California.)

> Christian home wants dependable girl. Light housework and care for children, ages 11, 8 and 6. (And an address in Las Vegas, Nevada.)

> WANTED: Mother's helper to live-in. 3 children. Nice home in Agoura, California. Permanent. Transportation provided.

> WANTED: Responsible and neat girl to live in, qualified for child care for school-age children and housework. $25 per week. (And an address in New York.)

For reasons that are unaccountable, my eyes settle on this ad:

> *Help Wanted*: Live-in housekeeper and loving baby-sitter for 3 children, ages 8, 5 and 3 years old. Room and board plus $25 a week to start. Transportation paid to Irvine, Calif. Must at least stay a year. No smoking. (And there's a number to call. Collect.)

I sit in my motel room, staring at the phone and pondering what to say.

What about my accent? Might the person answering the phone recognize that I don't sound like a Navajo? I convince myself that the average Anglo doesn't know that much about Navajos.

What about the language? I know only a few words, not enough to pass inspection, should she, my new employer, know Navajo. I console myself that the possibility is remote. There are many Navajos who can't speak their own language. My friend Wilma Veres is a full-blooded Navajo, and she doesn't speak Navajo. And then I recall lunching one day with Wilma and twelve other Indians who were attending a conference on alcoholism. Each Indian represented a different tribe, and each spoke a distinct dialect—and could only converse with one another in English. I decide that should I be asked to speak Navajo I would claim one of the more esoteric Indian dialects, such as Taramara.

Other doubts begin to assail me. What if my new white employer thinks I look too light-skinned to be a Navajo? Might I then respond that my grandfather, or even my father, was white? I have met many Navajos with white grandfathers. Bessie Yellowhair, for instance. And like the real Miss Yellowhair, my hair also is dark.

What about my name? Certainly my name doesn't sound very Indian to an Anglo who is fascinated by descriptive names such as Hardbelly, Wife Beater, Black Elk and Red Fox. But thousands of Indians were given Anglo names by white traders and white schoolteachers, and I have met full-blooded Navajos who are called Jones, Brown, and Smith.

Still I am reluctant to use my real name, for fear the woman in California might have heard of my *Soul Sister* experience. Bessie Yellowhair has given me permission to use her name, and though I am loath to involve her if anything goes wrong, I can't think of anything better, and when I make the call I identify myself as "Bessie Yellowhair."

"Oh, yes, Betsy—Betsy YELLOW?" the woman replies as if mentally making a note for herself. I don't correct her.

Has she filled the job? I ask.

"No, I've talked with some girls." She rattles on in a rather disorganized fashion, repeating that she doesn't have her "list of questions" handy.

"Betsy, do you know how to run a vacuum sweeper?" Yes.

"Do you *like* children?" Yes.

All of her questions seem designed to elicit an easy yes response. Deliberately, I avoid any more than curt replies. I give her the Indian treatment; she asks a question, I answer, then fall silent. She struggles to fill up the void, and I get the feeling she is less interested in me as a person, a human being, than as a commodity to be fitted into her household.

"We have three *lovely* children," she tells me, insisting that she knows I will just love them. At this point, her tone of voice, sweetly maternalistic, almost prompts my confession: this is a sham on my part, but you are so good

—and I know your children are so *lovely*—I will work for you for nothing! Yes, yes, *yes*.

The woman, who never reveals her name, says they live in a two-story house and I would live upstairs in a room with Jeffie, the three-year-old. "I've put a chest in there, in his closet," she says. She has bought a cot, she hastens to add, and then wonders aloud if it will accommodate me. Has she perhaps seen a photograph of an enormously fat squaw and identified all Indians with that image?

"Betsy, about this cot—" and she frankly admits she doesn't know how to frame the question, but she blurts it out: "Just how big are you?"

It's the first question I can't answer with a yes. I lapse into a silence as I struggle for an answer, reflecting that in Turkey where men really appreciate large buttocks and bodies I'm not big enough, but when I go to a health club in America, where women strive to be only bones, I am too big. Eventually I tell her: Not too big.

Then, with a hint of relief in her voice, she asks, "So you can fit on just an average cot?"

Yes.

Her audible sigh suggests I've met her number one qualification: not being overly fat.

Her next question: "Have you had experience in this type of work before?"

I think of all the floors I've mopped, the furniture I've dusted. *Once a friend said, "There's not a lazy bone in your body." And I remember my mother, not a lazy bone in her body. She never complained about work, washing sheets, scrubbing floors. Mother, let me help you. "No," she'd say, "this is what I like to do."*

"Have you ever done this type of work?" the woman in California repeats.

Yes.

Again, she seems vastly relieved to get that answer.

I get a sinking sensation that I'm about to fall heir to the problems of a "modern mother," who wants to consign her responsibilities to a trustworthy hired hand, that I am to be the ultimate in labor-saving devices.

"Do you have children?" she asks.

No.

"And, Betsy—do you know where Irvine is?"

Hmm. Is it close to Los Angeles?

She responds with a quiz master's enthusiasm: "Yes. So you've heard of Los Angeles, that's good, Betsy."

Again, my silence. Is she putting me on? How can she possibly think me that dumb?

But then I realize I am no longer *me*; *I* do not exist at all. I am now existing—*as an Indian*—but *only in the mind* of this woman. I turn over enormous powers to her: my psychic self. I have, in a way, gotten rid of myself.

She asks me to call her back the same time tomorrow. When I hang up a morbid depression envelops me. Psychologists tell us a state of depression usually comes when one experiences a great sense of loss. What have I lost? My name, I have given away my name.

The next day I call.

"Yes, Betsy, we've decided we want you." And she says she'll prepay a bus ticket to Santa Ana from Holbrook.

It would be easier for me to go from Gallup, I tell her.

"No, I've talked with other people. They always prepay the ticket from Holbrook," she tells me. She makes me feel I'm not a person, but merely part of a plan.

I suspect there's some kind of agency that advises people how to get cheap live-in Indian help direct from the reservation. The bus ticket costs twenty-five dollars from Holbrook to California, but since there are *no* public conveyances that operate within Navajoland, there's no bus that I can take from Window Rock to Holbrook. Even

Bessie, with all of her clan family, had to depend on an Anglo, the priest who got her the job, to drive her to Holbrook.

I think of my alternatives. The easy Anglo way would be to pay someone to drive me to Holbrook, a distance of 120 miles from the Navajo capital. But as "Bessie Yellowhair," I feel it ridiculous to pay someone half a week's salary to get me to my embarkation station. My only other alternative is to hitchhike to Holbrook.

I reflect on all the Navajos that I've picked up in my drives over the reservation. Now, I decide, turnabout is fair play. I will be the one needing the ride. I feel confident that I can get a ride—probably I will need several. But you never know how long you'll have to stand there. The bus from Holbrook to Santa Ana leaves at 6 P.M., so I plan to get on the highway by 6 A.M., to allow twelve hours for hitchhiking to Holbrook.

Now as I begin preparations to "pass" as an Indian, I feel more lost than I ever felt as a "black" woman. My *Soul Sister* experiences were always, at the core, akin to going home. Nothing black was alien to me, not crawling into Mrs. Tubbs' bed, not eating turnip greens, least of all the experience of going to church with blacks. I was going back "home" in the sense that with the blacks I returned to my religious beliefs. All blacks and whites are under the one umbrella of the Judeo-Christian ethic. We all believe in those "gods" of industry and cleanliness and good cars.

When I turned "black," I learned to feel that spiritually I was black, and today I feel black as well as white.

But spiritually—can I ever feel Indian?

In *Soul Sister*, I kept my name and darkened my skin.

In this instance, I keep my skin—and change my name. The prospect is challenging, and a little frightening. As "Bessie Yellowhair" I feel I am permanently abandoning myself; that I have to submerge, if not eradicate, all that I have been. And I am uncertain about making the psychological adjustment. I grope for the rationalizations that will sustain me. The job will *not* be permanent. I will not feel as "locked in" as Bessie did, I can cope with this *a little while*. I tell myself that I can recapture my *white birthright* at will. But, I struggle to jettison all notions of a masquerade. I must walk across a threshold of altered identity as thoroughly bereft of my white self as possible. I am obliged to try to see it as "Bessie" would.

As an Anglo visiting the reservation, I brought as few things as possible. But even so, I have far too many clothes and accessories. Now, I must in a sense unpack, not pack, for my journey. The recollection of Bessie arriving at her job with only the clothes she wore prods me to be austere.

For my *Soul Sister* experience, I did not give much thought to packing for trips as a "black" woman to Harlem and Mississippi. Since blacks and whites wear the same clothes, I merely packed a bag, as for most any trip. And when I began living among black women in Harlem I found that they had possessions similar to those I carried, except more of them, in many cases.

Then when I got a room in Mississippi, a shriveled black janitor encountering me in a hall said, "You don't have *nothing* in that room." He had inspected it thoroughly and reminded me I didn't have a gun, TV or stockings. He read into my few possessions a need, a need of him. He could help me, he said, meaning help me get *things*.

I turn the car back to the rental agency. I package all my identification cards and mail them to Washington. Should a policeman stop me in a bus station or when I am walking down a street, or when I am working in California, and ask: What are you doing here? Who are you?—

What will I say? I feel stripped, cast into a helpless anonymity.

I can no longer produce my "preferential" cards. Nor a driver's license, checkbook, pocket wallet, address and phone book.

One day, I know, I will want to make an escape. Inside my undergarments I sew two coins and a five-dollar bill.

Adrift and rudderless, I am besieged with a nagging doubt: what can this venture prove? My mind plays tricks on me. Suppose I can't make it back? What if I have made an irrevocable judgment and am permanently saddled with it? I seek solace from Thoreau: not till we are lost do we begin to understand ourselves. Now, once fully committed, I feel a gradual sense of calm, of letting go. Still, I am obsessed by what others will see. Strip a Cabinet official or even a President of his nice suit of clothes, take away his title and put him behind a wheel driving a cab. Would his philosophy of life be worth listening to? Would you even notice him, "see" him as a distinctive individual? Would he be any less faceless than an average cabdriver? Let his hair grow and put him in sandals and faded denim. Another vagrant, you'd say.

Now my shoes, stockings, dresses, I lay aside. My wardrobe is reduced to what a Navajo woman wears.

6 A.M. I leave the motel. I carry the flowered canvas suitcase, and walk from the motel to Highway 264 that goes to Tuba City. I have previously headed west, but always in the driver's seat, and quite willing to pick up hitchhikers. Had I thought then that I might be in their shoes? I can't remember. Already I begin to forget the time when I had a different name.

Standing in the long fluted calico skirt, the dark maroon velveteen shirt, my hair in two pigtails and partially covered by a kerchief tied securely around my head, I feel the whoosh of an occasional vehicle, and wonder why you rarely realize the speed of automobiles until they pass you on an open road.

When a pickup truck pulls off the road, kicking pebbles into my face, I lift my fluted skirt and run, carrying the flowered suitcase, and climb into the front seat beside a man with an old, tarnished look to his skin, and I am distressed to realize that he is *not like me*. He is not a Navajo, *not one of us*, and I do not trust him. My adjustment is already taking hold. His assumption of superiority, and with it, an unmistakable disdain, diminishes my morale. I push myself against the door, fearing his intention.

"Where are you heading?" he asks in English.

Holbrook, I reply. I want to say more, but my voice gives way to a fear of betrayal. My will seems suddenly eroded, and instinctively I throw up my guard against a vaguely felt threat. My voice comes in slow motion and it is altogether detached from this other person, the one that I was, before.

"When we get there you can spend the night with me," he says in a casual but husky tone.

No, no, I tell him, and my shock is not at hearing his words so much as recognizing that I am almost defenseless. His truck is now going at least seventy miles an hour. This matter-of-factness is demoralizing, and I have to assert my resentment lest I encourage and embolden him. I recall that when I started to school I walked a distance of several miles, and one afternoon a tarnished old man, who looked very much like the driver of this pickup truck, stopped to offer me a ride. Driving me toward home, he reached a long arm over and put his hand up my skirt. With the fierceness of a wild animal, I turned on him, commanding—*You stop this car immediately! And let me out!* And somehow frightened by my strong voice and my courage, he stopped.

Now, where is my voice? I briefly ponder what Bessie

Yellowhair might do in this same situation. Then I hear myself saying—"You stop this car. You let me out!" Not so strong or so fierce as I would wish. But he does not argue. He insults me further with a snicker, as if he is merely amusing his whims by obeying my instructions. He pulls off the road and without either of us saying another word, I get out.

Standing alone again, the pickups and cars whizzing by, I try to recapture my sense of picaresque adventure. I have always traveled around by myself; but I have always had *me*, Grace.

Mrs. Yellowhair was right. Having experienced the closeness of a Navajo family, I now feel my aloneness more acutely. Now I have such an urge to flee—to run to a man as woman eternally has run to a man, begging: make a demand of me, demand that I be "true"—let me live in the demand that *you*, not I, make of myself. God, I pay a price not to live like a trinket on a man's watch chain.

Almost two hours pass. I still have a hundred miles to go. Another pickup stops. The driver is a young woman. I presume she is Navajo although from her dress—tight pants, loose shirt, and very short, mannish haircut—she could "pass" for Anglo. She has newspapers and magazines beside her, and her radio is tuned to the early morning news, in English.

I stare at two emblems: a statue of Christ glued to the dashboard and a United States flag decal plastered on the windshield. I reflect on the irony of our "roles." She— the good, red-blooded, flag-waving Christian American— wishes to "communicate," asking me if I have a family in Holbrook. I feel a surging melancholia, and sit silent, the "wooden" Indian. In my silence I say: do not try to be kind to me, you have done all that you can do by offering this ride. As to the rest, leave me alone.

We pass Ganado and the Project Hope hospital where

Bessie works, and go on to Steamboat. Then my driver
lets me out at the intersection of Highways 264 and 77,
she continues west toward Tuba City, and I stand by the
highway that leads due south to Holbrook.

It is now about noon. I have brought a couple of apples
along with me, and I munch on these while looking ahead
to one of the loneliest stretches of empty land that the eye
can see. The land that I must travel before nightfall
stretches out interminably. I am dwarfed by this space,
an inconsequential transient. God in His Heaven probably
couldn't find me in all this nothingness.

Eventually another pickup truck stops. The cab is filled
with six adult Navajos—probably the third one from the
driver must do the shifting—and the back section contains
almost a dozen children. I climb up with the children, and
we take off. One child, about four, inspects me, getting
about one inch from my face, and continues to stare at me
incredulously. And I tell her, in Spanish, that she is *muy
bonita, muy bonita.* I want her to feel as confused as I do.
Eventually, we get to Holbrook. The pickup truck stops
at the main intersection and I jump off and walk to the
bus station.

At the Holbrook station a drunken Indian approaches
me, slobbering in a barely coherent manner. He tells me
he and I should leave—together.

When I first came out to the reservation, I never saw a
man "look" at me, but now that I place myself in a defenseless position, alone on the road, I am seen as available, compliant, usable. I can't say "attractive." But what
makes a woman "attractive" to a man, her availability?
Her receptiveness? Her vulnerability? Obviously, the
drunken Indian has seen me as a handy pickup, a usable
commodity. So did the white driver of the pickup truck.

I walk to the ticket window, and from behind his
counter, a harassed, preoccupied white man looks at me
without interest. The man is perhaps fifty. Was he stand-

ing here handing out prepaid tickets for poverty-stricken Indians when the other Bessie Yellowhair left on a bus from Holbrook?

My name is Bessie Yellowhair—I dissemble. Does he have a prepaid ticket for me? I stand, almost holding my breath. Without hesitation, he turns to a stack of envelopes and, flipping through them casually, comes to one that's marked "Betsy Yellow." He marks in his ledger "no identification," and without ever speaking a word, hands me the ticket. I am left to wonder if none of the poor Indian women who accept prepaid tickets to white households ever carry identifications. In any case, I have "passed" for a Navajo—with no proof, other than my appearance, required.

The westbound bus is late; I walk outside to breathe some fresher air, to make sure that my legs have not grown weak. The drunken Indian who accosted me earlier weaves his way outside and leans against the wall to avoid falling. He slides up and down the wall, and then topples and lies prone, "dead" drunk. Other passengers, coming and going, step around him the way you'd step around a garbage can, without even seeing it.

While I have traveled much, without hellos or goodbyes, I now yearn for someone to see me off, to hold my hand, reassure me.

I finger the bracelet Bessie Yellowhair has loaned me. My only talisman.

Now what I feel is a kind of "death"—a nothingness, a giving over to the plan, as to a malady.

I remember, lying ill, waiting for my body to take over and cure itself of serum hepatitis. Only time is master; I must submit, totally.

* * *

On the bus, Holbrook to California: Twenty-five years
ago I bought a ticket as long as your two outstretched
arms, which, if memory serves, cost about eighteen dollars, and boarded a Greyhound in Fort Worth. It wasn't
a wayward bus, but my itinerary was delightfully aimless
as we rode across Texas and New Mexico and Arizona,
and one midnight I stumbled off in Los Angeles, got a
hotel room, rested overnight and then took a sightseeing
"bus-tour" of the city. Then on to San Francisco and Salt
Lake City, writing picture postcards home all the way. It
was pure adventure for me, with few apprehensions and
no remembered fears.

Now, in my Bessie Yellowhair attire, I briefly relive
other bus rides, through Malaysia, Mexico and Madrid to
Malaga. I always felt—as a wide-eyed reporter who asked
pertinent questions and wrote down impertinent answers
—that I could go wherever I wanted to go, that the world
was an unrestricted province for the inquisitive, venture-
some traveler.

On those earlier bus rides, I managed to sit up front,
behind the driver, and although a sign above him said,
"Driver not allowed to talk with passengers," it was no
trick to draw him into conversation. As a somewhat tense
and taciturn "Bessie Yellowhair," though, I occupy a seat
farther back in the bus, yet close enough to be within
earshot of an inquisitive young girl who queries the driver
and with pad and pencil in hand jots down his replies.

We pass a series of huge, grotesque billboards touting
the "Indian Village" ahead, and I hear the driver saying:

"They get tourists in there and sell them a bunch of
junk. One tourist bought an 'Indian' blanket for eighty
dollars and then learned it was made in Pendleton, Oregon. And the 'Indian' beads are made in Japan."

He points out the turnoffs for the Painted Desert and
the Grand Canyon. When we stop in Winslow, Arizona,

the station is closed for the night but a cluster of passengers wait outside. I notice four white adults and I see two Indian youths, who might be college students. They have been sitting on a bench, drinking cans of beer. The driver steps off the bus, takes the tickets from the whites. The Indian youths approach with their tickets, but the hefty driver shoves them aside with a force that leaves them staggering, almost falling.

"No drunk Indians on my bus!" he barks.

He climbs back behind the wheel, and closes the door with sullen authority. As he starts the motor I look from my window seat into the faces of the youths, faces filled with anger and frustration; rebellious, yet *hopeless* faces.

I recall a *Soul Sister* experience, when I was waiting for a bus among a group of blacks in Jackson, Mississippi. A white city bus driver stopped and then, although his bus was half-empty, suddenly gunned his motor and drove past, derisively laughing at his prank on us "niggers." I was then among blacks of my own generation who Uncle Tommed and showed no reaction to that familiar gesture of contempt. The black youth of today are something else.

When our bus pulled into Winslow, a cluster of loud teen-aged black girls disembarked, and one, for no apparent reason, exclaimed—"SHEE—EET!" Then taunted the bus driver, "Lookee here at this nice *gentle* man, helping me off this bus!" And her companions laughed while the huge driver looked intimidated as only a black woman can make a white man look these days. His passivity contrasted markedly with his rude treatment of the Indians.

The bus rolls on. I stare into a maze of glaring, garish neons that intrude harshly on the night sky and stars. They beckon the traveler into a series of motels that seemingly stretch without end from Arizona to California. I see long, shining cars pull into the motels, all with restaurants and bars and swimming pools. One sign boldly

punctuates my odd sense that beyond the bus line lies
Babylon:

HAVE YOUR AFFAIR HERE

I see millions of wasted kilowatts and think of the
hogan, without electricity. And yet our government has
condoned the use of Navajo lands for more power plants
to supply consumers here, who will place bigger and more
flashing signs:

KING-SIZED BEDS
WATER BEDS AVAILABLE

In Los Angeles, I must change buses. The information
booth is closed. People swarm about as in Grand Central
on a holiday. It takes all of my resolve and energy to find
how one locates the bus to Santa Ana. What would the
real Bessie Yellowhair have done? I remember with a
new sympathy her account of how lost and lonely she had
felt. I, worldly traveler, feel that I've never been off the
reservation. I am insecure, nervous and *assaulted*—by the
noise, confusion, frustration of thousands who are frantic
to get wherever they must go.

A kind porter tells me to wait at Gate 14. I wait two
hours, and eventually the bus to Santa Ana materializes
like a reluctant blessing.

Counting my time hitchhiking and waiting for buses,
I have been traveling thirty hours when the Greyhound
rolls alongside a brick station in Santa Ana. With my
exhaustion comes a kind of indifference. I see a white
woman with a small boy standing outside, obviously waiting for a passenger. By now, in previous stops along the
way, all the other "Indians" have left the bus. When I
step off, carrying Bessie Yellowhair's flowered canvas bag,
and dressed in Bessie Yellowhair's clothes, the woman
easily identifies me.

"You must be Betsy!" And turning she prods her young son, "Jeffie, here's Betsy. Our new girl. Say hello to Betsy."

Jeffie, three, looks glum, stares at his shoes. Why, indeed, should *he* acknowledge me, when his mother has convinced him I am less than a sovereign human being? Isn't she deliberately demeaning "Betsy" when she does not say—"I am Mrs. so and so" and *shake hands with me?*

My employer, in her late thirties, is dressed casually. She has a large nose and mouth, and wears dark sunshades. She is tall, clean cut, attractive, with a long, sturdy pared-down frame. She wears her short brown hair in a casual cut, and she keeps staring down at Jeffie until eventually he gloomily responds:

"Hullo, Betsy."

As we start off, she reveals her "goodness," to herself, at least:

"I had a woman coming for four days a week. But I got rid of her *because of you*." She speaks in tones of calculated sweetness and solicitude. Betsy, she is saying in effect, YOU MUST MEASURE UP.

Listening to her voice I am disconcerted; I have heard it before, in Mississippi, where I worked as a "black" maid for just such a woman, whose falsely sweet words concealed her patronizing attitude.

Suddenly, we hear frantic screams from Jeffie, who, despite our having driven some distance, wants to be returned to the Greyhound station. "Mommee, I didn't wave good-bye to the bus!" Now it's his turn for one-upmanship. His mother turns, we drive to the station, and Jeffie waves to the empty bus.

"We have the three most lovable children," she says. "Betsy, I know you will adore them."

I am silent, and this alarms her.

"Betsy, you do like children? You said you liked children?"

Yes, I say.

"Do you have sisters?" she asks. It is the first personal question, concerning me and not her, she has asked.

"How many sisters?" she asks.

Three, I say.

We are now on a freeway, and I lose all sense of direction. I feel that I have become an answering machine, with replies dictated by uncontrollable circumstances. An ambulance with a near-deafening siren screams by, and I hear Bessie Yellowhair saying, "My head was always spinning with the noise." Coming from the reservation my ears now seem more sensitive to the urban sounds that force up one's blood pressure, tense muscles, frazzle nerves.

"Oh, Betsy," my employer is saying, "I meant to tell you on the phone. You must stay a year."

I do not know how to respond, and I feel my willpower and self-assertiveness flowing out of me, as if I have just been bled to the point of total, irrevocable submissiveness.

I recall Bessie Yellowhair telling me of a movie, *Planet of the Apes*, in which men teach apes to do menial jobs; Bessie said the trained apes had reminded her of her experiences as an Indian domestic in California. "I felt like a slave," she told me. Now, because I have given enormous powers to this woman, allowing her to say I *must* stay a year, I feel physically trapped; and I can more readily understand how Bessie became convinced that a white woman had the right to "buy" an Indian girl for a year.

My employer assumes my silence means total acceptance of her will.

"Betsy, that's good, then we can count on you to stay a year! That's *real* good.

"Now," she continues, "about your sisters—I have a lovely neighbor, and she needs a girl. Maybe one of your sisters will come out? I'm only suggesting this for *your* welfare. This way, *you* won't be so lonely."

She insists on knowing if I can persuade a sister to come.

No, I tell her, I didn't think so.

"What about some of your friends? *You* need another Indian out here so *you* won't be lonely," she tells me. "I'm only thinking of you."

I have been expecting her to ask me about my skin, my accent, my Indian-ness, but she obviously does not "see" me; she sees only the old clothes that Bessie Yellowhair has loaned me, and she sees that she can twist me as easily as putty.

Not once has she indicated any interest in the land from which I've come. Once, casually, she had asked, "How's the weather *out there?*"—making the "out there" sound too remote to engage her attention.

Leaving the expressway, we turn toward a new housing development, and my eye scans a billboard informing me that Irvine—83,000 acres, 130 square miles—is "full of fun. And games." We pass a Walnut Village of $29,000 homes . . . Greentree Homes . . . President Homes . . . Harbor View Homes . . . then Spyglass Hill homes, all in the $80,000 range. I reflect that $80,000 would support eighty Indian families for a year.

I do not see "life" around me, only great expanses of lawn and impressive layers of brick and moving automobiles. I long for the streets of Harlem! For the flow of humanity. This development seems planned out of existence, dead, more frightening—with the look-alike houses for look-alike whites—than our so-called crime-infested streets. But the designers here have probably won prizes for their conception of Arcadia.

We arrive at a two-story house built of California red-wood in the $35,000-price range. My new employer parks her station wagon in the drive of a double garage, opens a wooden gate onto a small patio, and we pass through a sliding glass door into the den-kitchen.

Jeffie retrieves his kiddy-car from the patio, pedals in on our heels and scoots over my feet. Two other children run in, boisterously.

"Sandy, Dave, this is our new girl, this is Betsy, you must mind Betsy.

"And, Betsy"—the mother turns to me—"you must never let Jeffie out of your sight; Sandra and David must always ask your permission when they go out. You must *at all times* know where they are."

Taking a tight hold on myself in this surreal scene, I struggle to distinguish Dave from Jeffie and Sandy. I feel sluggish and slightly disoriented. Perhaps the long bus ride, the uncertainty of my new role have led to my sense of near-terror. *Steady, steady,* an inner voice counsels. My body rhythms seem still attuned to a moving vehicle. I concentrate on my new wards.

Sandy, a thin girl of eight, appears nervous, while David, a dark-haired boy of five, strikes me as extremely small for his age, not much larger than three-year-old Jeffie.

Their mother's attitude toward Betsy, the "Indian," has the effect of diminishing me in the children's eyes, and I am psychologically shrunken, not an infant and not yet an adult. The children perceive me as someone to be tested, if not tyrannized.

"Betsy, may I have a marshmallow?"

"Betsy, I'm going to the playground, okay?"

Testing, testing, the will of a child against that of an adult, or rather, against that of an "Indian" girl.

Adult or *girl*, I feel suddenly outnumbered and out-maneuvered, while the mother, like a spectator at a sports contest, watches with obvious enjoyment as I parry the badgering, wary and defensive. Eventually she turns referee.

"After Betsy gives you your lunch, *then* she will decide." And with a note of finality she instructs me: "You must keep your eye on them constantly; if anything happens to any one of them, *you* are responsible."

The thought crosses my mind that I've just witnessed a well-rehearsed retirement ceremony for one who has deliberately, and with a great sense of relief, relinquished all duties. But in almost the same instant, I realize with mounting dismay that I have inherited those duties and responsibilities, and that henceforth I am captain of a ship manned by a potentially mutinous crew.

Her desperation to rid herself of a mother's responsibility puzzles me, especially since I am a stranger for whom she has revealed no respect, only a kind of benign disdain as an unfeeling domestic. She has not even told me her name, nor reached out to me in any way. She did not take my hand at the bus station or make any gesture to allay any misgivings I might be suffering.

If I had been a sister, a relative, or even a casual acquaintance, I might comprehend her abrupt abdication and the naming of me as a kind of executor of her children's fortunes. But we haven't been in the house five minutes!

The mother has told me I'll share a room with Jeffie, and now she says: "I'll show you where to leave your bag."

As we start up the stairs, I am startled by a man, obviously her husband, on the top landing, surveying us glumly. He is tall, about forty, deeply tanned, in white tennis attire. His feet are wide apart, his arms folded across his chest. He seems to be staring at me, and I quickly discern hostility in his posture. But he isn't "seeing" me, and the anger toward his wife is thinly veiled.

"Angel, how many days have you left the stereo running?"

The term "angel" somehow conveys more contempt than had he called her an unseemly name.

Disconcerted, I pause midway on the steps.

"This is Betsy!" his wife shouts.

He ignores the "introduction," and in the same accusatory tone, says: "The machine is hot, it must have been running *for days.*"

They argue briefly, the wife claiming that Mary, the former maid, must have left the machine running.

"She was told *never* to turn it on!" he storms.

I feel helplessly embarrassed by their scene, and wonder if it is a common one. I also wonder about the children—how often they might be subjected to this petty bickering.

She has told me that her husband is an engineer and well organized and thoughtful. Now I listen to him rant, wholly unconcerned about the impression his behavior might have on me. "Inferior" Indian or not, I have been assigned the task of caring for his children, and yet he remains indifferent, not only to me but to what I might think about the head of the household.

The wife and I go into Jeffie's room, and the husband goes down the steps and onto a community green that serves a dozen or more adjoining homes.

Through open windows, I hear the husband's voice, introducing himself to a new neighbor—"I'm Bob Morton," and then he adds that he's an engineering consultant, identifying himself with his job, as if the two were one. And laughing—"Just think of bulldozers when you think of me." Thinking now as "Bessie Yellowhair," I am appalled.

My new employer takes me on a tour of the house, giv-

ing me explicit instructions along the way about how
to wash windows, mop and wax floors, polish furniture.
Everything is functional. Her home is as convenient as a
TraveLodge and about as inviting. I long for a comfortable
chair, a cozy nook in which to collapse with a book or a
magazine. But there's an unlived quality here, as if the
rooms and furniture were part of a model house, arranged
with a functional tidiness to account for everything except
real live people.

When I return to the room I will share with Jeffie, I feel
cramped, in a way I never felt in the hogan. Yet by com-
parison, this house is unbelievably luxurious. I feel this
room is closing in on me. A hogan, twenty feet in dimen-
sion, accommodates fourteen Navajos quite adequately,
but it has little but a stove and sleeping space, while the
living space of this room has been dissipated by furnish-
ings, clothes, toys—an overabundance of belongings.

Jeffie at three already has as many personal effects as a
Navajo accumulates in a lifetime. David has more than
Jeffie and Sandy has more than David. One Anglo concept
has been that you live in proportion to your possessions.

When we go into the master bedroom with its king-sized
bed, Mrs. Morton emphasizes a rule: "The kids are never
allowed in our room." Her words sadden and confuse me.
I have come to think like the Navajo: that in a family one
puts others, not himself, first, that the parents "love" one
another by working and providing and sacrificing for their
children, and, since they love their children, the young are
always close to their parents. I recall seeing a Navajo child
the age of Jeffie going to his mother's arms and her opening her blouse and nursing him; though one could not be
sure there was milk for the child, one could be sure there
was love.

After introducing me to a massive array of bleaches,
waxes, polishes—I had not seen a greater assortment of

"miracle" cleaners on the housekeepers' shelves at the White House in Washington—Mrs. Morton sits with me in the den-kitchen, and gives me a list of her rules and regulations:

House

Each morning: straighten house, make beds, clean rooms
    (check clothes)
clean kitchen, clothes to service porch, keep stove and
    formica clean
vacuuming—
    rugs, Kirby, set at 2 or 3
    vinyl floors—whirlpool
    do runners (sliding doors)
    furniture in living room (once a month)
mopping, vinyl cleaning—then clear water

Weekly

Monday, ironing
Tuesday, dusting, vacuum (upstairs) lemon oil (once a
    month)
Wednesday, washing/folding   bathrooms   clean refriger-
    ator   washer/dryer
Thursday, windows, change beds, mirrors
Friday, washing/folding   vacuum (downstairs)
Saturday, dusting, mop
Sunday, washing/folding

   Once a Month:

       wipe down bar stools and chairs
       wipe down woodwork in kitchen
       clean oven and hood over stove
       pine sol Jeffie's crib—pediatric table

pine sol Dave's bed
clean shower (floor glass—inside and out)
wipe down black couch and chair

Children Care
  KIDS

Food schedule—see menu; breakfast, 7–7:30, snack
  10 (only fruit, veg., raisins) lunch, 12–1, snack 3
  (only fruit, veg., raisins) dinner, 5–7. Walks, Jeffie
  to play lots, 10:30–11:30; Sandy and Jeffie 3:30–
  4:30 play in the park, visit friends
Jeffie needs to be watched over completely
Sandy and David should let it be known where they
  are at all times and should check in periodically
Eating—kids are to eat at the table or bar *not* in any
  other part of the house
Clothes—keep clean and neat (any holes or repairs
  needed—put in sewing basket)
    Dress warm or cool according to weather
    Early morning—late afternoon—sweaters
    Change between naps if dirty
    Clean out shoes and cuffs if played in sand
    Kids should be clean when coming in house

Jeffie and Sandy should sit at table and draw, color,
  write sometime each day
Play in house—kids are not to have friends in to play
  in their rooms. Play outside or downstairs only.
  Quiet play—cards etc.

No rough playing—no running in the house. No chas-
  ing, hide and seek, running on stairs, playing near
  windows.
No drawing, coloring anywhere but table and desk

Kids not allowed in our room

No standing on furniture

Jeffie—check on going potty, especially after breakfast, and before nap. He shouldn't play in other kids' rooms

Kids not allowed to get into any cupboards
　　Not to get any games down or touch the medicine

Medicine—vitamins—you will give—kids never to touch it

Help kids with their chore list

Temperature should not go above 65 in the daytime

Jeffie *must be, has to be* watched every minute. Can't be left unattended

Jeffie's temperature—if it goes above 102 he must have phenobarbital

Jeffie—nap 1:00–3:00

The Mortons are mixing cocktails in the kitchen. I have supper ready for the children and lift Jeffie into a high chair, but drop the chair's detachable tray. Morton rushes over and picks up the tray. "Betsy!" he scolds. "This is very simple, even *a little child* can attach this. Now watch." And before my eyes can focus on his handiwork, he has the tray back on the chair.

Morning: An alarm sounds at seven. I hear the humming of Morton's electric razor, and then his electric shoe shiner, and I overhear Mrs. Morton's concern about her shoes matching her suit.

I clean and dress the children, getting Sandra ready for school; the parents go downstairs and prepare their coffee and toast. When the children and I come downstairs, she has told me, she and her husband will be ready to walk out the door for their jobs. Their split-second timing contrasts sharply with life in the hogan, where figures move silently, unclocked, unhurried, almost as if in slow motion.

Morton is still in the kitchen when I herd the children in for their breakfast. I get Jeffie seated in his high chair. I feel the father's intense gaze on me. Perhaps I am trying too hard, but I fumble and drop the tray.

"Betsy! I never saw anyone so dumb!" he shouts harshly. "Can't you ever learn!"

Since our self-esteem tends to depend on what others think of us, I am depreciated and depressed by the remark, even feeling it justified. I can sympathize with Rosemary Yellowhair's appraisal of herself as "retarded" after a white instructor placed her in a class for retarded students. And if I stay here a year, won't I in fact become the "dumb Betsy" Morton presumes me to be? My self-respect is draining from me.

In my *Soul Sister* experience, working as a "black" maid, I encountered white men who lusted for me, betraying their desire to assault me—*physically*. My blackness made me "different" and actually desirable in their eyes. Now that I am an "Indian" woman, the white man sees me as "different," too, but not in a lustful way. Instead, he seems passionately desirous of assaulting me—*mentally*.

Is there a penance factor here? Do I, as an Indian, representing a different lifestyle, a drastically different ethic, instill doubts in him about the virtues of his lifestyle and ethic? Does he fear that if he does not diminish my mind I will tear off his ceremonial mask that hides him from himself? Vine Deloria has said that "until non-Indian peoples understand themselves and the religion they profess to confess, the situation of the American Indians will grow continually worse."

Morton leaves in his car seconds after Mrs. Morton has sped off in her station wagon. She has told me she works in a bank. In her fast footwork to beat her husband out of the door I see she wants a home, husband, children—and no responsibilities. Driving in from the bus station she kept insisting she had three "lovable," children and she knew I would "adore" them, but as lovable and adorable as they may be, she neglects them for the money at the bank.

Sandra, who is ready for school, reminds me that David must take his special medicine at mid-morning, and that Jeffie is ready to "toidy." Then she adds, "He gets a reward if he does good."

I ask: What did she mean, "does good?"

"If he does it average he gets a penny and if he does a lot my mother gives him a nickel." Some Navajos believe money is the means by which Anglos measure all of life. Sandy continues, "I have a nickel to give him, if he does good."

We place Jeffie in position and like a track star urged to get on your mark, ready, set—Go!—he seems to understand the challenge.

We leave the boy to his own devices, but then almost immediately he calls for inspection. Sandra runs in and I follow, and she tells him he did "good"—and I see he's been programmed into nothing short of diarrhea.

On the reservation the Indians are reticent about their bowel movements. They simply vanish into the space surrounding them, and relieve themselves. I never knew where they went, and nothing was ever said about it. And they have a fetish about carefully covering or burying their waste. My living on the reservation has made the bowel habits of the Morton children almost obscene to me.

At mid-morning I remember I must give David a special medicine for a malady involving his nervous system. I go to the playground and ask him to return home with me.

He agrees reluctantly, but only after I insist it's his snack time.

When I offer him the medicine, he refuses to take it. When I insist, he slaps my wrist so furiously that the liquid spills to the floor. His belligerence stuns me. I know that children who feel they are unloved, unwanted, who are not caressed and hugged and kissed as infants and children, will have problems adjusting as adults.

I recall my own childhood sickness, and having to take a bitter medicine. My father would stand over me, fondly, and pour out a tablespoon of the bitter liquid and say, "Look, daughter, it is not bad—" and swallow the medicine himself, reassuring me and making my dose seem more palatable. I want to give David this kind of love, but I lack the devotion and, not knowing anything about the ingredients of his medicine, the courage.

Patiently, I emplore: Take it for me. After many entreaties, he finally agrees. I think of Bessie Yellowhair sitting by a young boy's bed when he was sick, attempting to comfort him. "And his mother was out partying," she remembered.

I do four runs of the washing machine, for different garments, the white, the colored, the drip-drys, the woolens. Each run requires a different detergent and a different speed. Some clothes I put in the dryer; others I take to a line in the patio.

I'm washing more clothes than the average Navajo family possesses in a lifetime.

I am obsessed with the amount of water and electricity that I use. With each wash, I compare the amount of water I've wasted to the amount an average Indian family uses.

In the hogan we all washed our faces and hands out of a community pan; no one poured out more than a cup of water at a time. We hung clothes outside, to be "dry cleaned" in the sun and air.

I am on my feet constantly, cleaning the house, rechecking the children's safety. And taking out small mountains of garbage. The contrast between our overabundant society and the spare subsistence life in the hogan must overwhelm the real Indian servant. This white family accumulates more waste materials in a day than hogan dwellers would in a period of several months. Navajos in a hogan have no collection of "junk" mail—there are no mail deliveries; no newspapers that stack up; and few if any bottled or canned goods. The meals are simple; and there are no leftovers. Whatever is cooked is eaten.

For the past two nights, the Mortons have invited neighboring couples in for dinner.

I have been busy with my chores, taking Jeffie out for walks, and then preparing and feeding the children their supper.

The first evening the father was in the kitchen preparing rum drinks called Mai-tais, and last evening he whipped up Margaritas. Unawares, I watched him, and even caught myself wondering at one point if I might be offered a taste, but I quickly reminded myself not to let my mind go wandering.

When the guests entered from the back sliding glass door into the kitchen, I had the distinct impression that they had come, partially, at least, to get an unveiling, as it were, of the newly arrived "Indian" from the reservation.

Seeing them staring at me, I recalled the dime I paid as a child to see a "real, live Indian" in a Lubbock, Texas, sideshow. In the ensuing decades, had the Anglos really changed so much?

While their guests gawked, Mrs. Morton said, by way of introduction—but never divulging the guests' names—"This is *our* Betsy."

"You like it here, Betsy?" one woman asked. But didn't wait for an answer, rushing on to another question, one that Mrs. Morton had already asked, about my sisters. This woman, too, wanted to know if I couldn't persuade a sister to come here and work. And she continued with the same line of persuasion. "Then you won't be so lonely, Betsy. Wouldn't that be nice?"

The "inspection" tour completed, the guests retired to the living room, where they enjoyed their drinks and later a buffet supper of beef burgundy over rice, with a side dish of salad.

I no longer believe in hours measured by minutes, in days measured by hours. I see no escape. I have found no time when I do not have full responsibility for the children.

When I passed as "black," I only did day work for white employers. A black servant working by the hour knows that however tedious the chores, a time comes when she can stop being a "slave" and return to a community of those who will replenish her spirit, strengthen her through love, for a new day. Now I am constantly forced to enact the role of "Betsy—Indian maid" for every waking moment. There is not one second when I have time to retreat to myself, and thus the real "me" has ceased to exist.

Saturday: The Mortons leave for the tennis courts, she very proud of herself with her long firm legs.

Later when they come in, he mixes drinks in the blendor. He serves her a Margarita and then, when she pours herself a second, he sternly reprimands:

"Hey! You're turning alcoholic! *Take it easy.*"

"You didn't 'take it easy' with me," she scoffs, alluding to some secret to which only they are privy. I presume she means in their game of tennis, but she could mean in the bedroom. I have learned from bits of conversation that she is again pregnant; and I feel certain that she isn't happy about it.

The Mortons are a competitive couple, subtly jousting with each other for small advantages in a game I never fully understand, but it is being played with a controlled toughness, without the soft edges of affection that one might expect in a youthful family.

He proudly boasts of "his" trophies won at various sports, and she has "her" emblems of triumph. One of the first questions Sandra asked me was: "Did you see my pennants?" She "won" them at swimming. Even the younger children are infected by the competitive tensions. David and Jeffie insist that I know they too have "won" at swimming. But a spirit of fun is lacking.

Good mental health, Freud believed, is based on the ability to love and to work. In this type of family, work has become an unpleasant means to make money and love appears a calculated act of procreation. If there's enjoyment in their games, it is concealed. I can't imagine either of my employers relaxing, letting go, just playing—for sheer pleasure.

How I long to trade my present situation for life back in the hogan. I miss people who come into the "home"—as simple as a mud hut may be—and are eager to relax and laugh at the ridiculous, incongruous and even obscene aspects of life. I miss the warmth, spontaneity, joy—that special intimacy of the unpretentious.

Late afternoon: The Mortons have gone to neighbors for drinks. Before leaving, she specifically told me to scrub the broiler, and she took it from the oven and left it in the sink.

I attack it vigorously. When I check on the children, I find Dave. And Sandra. But where's Jeffie? I again hear the mother's words: *"If anything happens to the children, you are responsible!*" And I am never to let Jeffie out of my sight."*He must be watched constantly.*"

I run to the playground but he's not there. A bit frantic, I hasten to a neighbor. No Jeffie. I age a year. And then out into the streets, where big and little cars move, strangely impersonal, in and out of the driveways. Panic mounts. The child! Where is Jeffie? My eyes fasten on the bumper stickers, as if they might provide a clue to his whereabouts: I'M THE GREATEST and DOWN WITH HOT PANTS! Then from behind one of the long parked cars, Jeffie appears riding calmly along on his miniature bicycle. I run to him, but I do not scold him; I take him in my arms, and, astonishingly, I am crying.

We return home just moments before the Mortons enter; he goes to his stereo and she walks to the oven and without asking about the children takes the broiler out and moves it over to the best light, over the sink, to inspect my cleaning job. I watch her drop the broiler in the sink, and snap, "Do this over!"

Almost mindlessly, I again scrub the broiler, recalling Bessie Yellowhair's account of a similar episode and how she had cried herself to sleep "because nobody had ever talked to me like that before." I remember her story of having ironed shirts all day only to have her employer tell her harshly, "Do these over!" As Bessie knew, it was not the work that "kills" you, but the deliberate effort to crush your spirit, to nullify your human-ness.

Too exhausted to sleep, I lie on my cot wondering if I am whole and human, speculating on how much more indignity I can tolerate. The idea of escape begins to absorb me. If I stay on, I will disintegrate. The thought of escape floats around me, like an apparition, but my will has been sapped, too. I have transformed myself into the helpless "Betsy" so completely that I feel enslaved, trapped, incapable of action.

The knowledge of my weakness paralyzes me even more.

I have been caught up in other experiences from which I felt there was no escape. Once, when I was traveling in the Amazonian rain forest, after days of jungle living, I came to feel imprisoned, beyond rescue, with only the giant river offering the hope of exit. I lapsed into a morbid mood, thinking that I had lived all my days in the jungle and would die there, estranged, undiscovered. Yet I was sustained by the conviction that I still possessed my soul and that no circumstances of organized society could rob me of it.

Now, I am not so sure. I have, momentarily, lost my grip, forgotten who I am or who I ever was. But like a hungry animal on the prowl I instinctively cling to the certainty that salvage is possible.

I have worked my mind into a melodramatic state, and am now persuaded that my way of life itself depends upon my getting out of this cot, and—yet, the thought of doing something of which the Mortons will disapprove immobilizes me. What strength it must have taken for an actual slave to escape.

My body moves. Once off the cot, I quickly slip into Bessie Yellowhair's skirt and overblouse; I pull on the white socks, the tennis shoes. I tie the old kerchief tightly around my head. I walk down the steps, cautious but determined. I do not know the hour, but it is still well before dawn. All quietness, except for the pounding of my heart. A deep fear is my companion. A conspiratorial sense of guilt troubles me. As the steps creak under my weight, I am slightly relieved to see the master's bedroom door is shut.

Stumbling through the darkened den-kitchen, I reach the sliding glass doors opening onto the patio. Before retiring, Mrs. Morton drew heavy damask drapes across the glass, and I fumble through the folds, searching for the lock. Oddly, in the utter blackness, my mind reruns the scene where Morton contemptuously called me "dumb," and the recollection adds to my nervousness. My hands are trembling as I locate the lock, but I can't work it open. Dumb Betsy! Morton would gloat.

After some moments I give up. I consider returning to my room. And stay here forever? The idea reinforces my resolve. I move as noiselessly as possible to the front door. It is a heavy, wooden door that creaks loudly when opened or closed.

I reach for the door knob, and—it turns! I try to mute the moan of the opening door. No time to be timid now, though. I hold my breath as I walk into the night air, and try to close the door without waking the family. But every sound is magnified in my ears, and I rein in my imagination. Would Morton, hearing his front door close, come lunging down the stairs, gun in hand, shouting, maybe even shooting?

Once out the door, I start to run, but as I round the house to go through the patio to the street, I collide with a cement pot for outdoor plants, and fall forward, breaking my weight with my arms. But I feel nothing as I get up quickly, and head for the street, walking rapidly and resolutely.

I walk for what seems like miles, passing row after row of curried lawns and those tidy development houses shielding a civilization of Mortons in their joyless security. At first, I long to see the lights of an automobile. When at length, lights appear, it occurs to me that any car cruising at this hour is likely to be a police car. I rush into a cluster of bushes, tearing my clothes, and throw myself in the dirt, exhausted, frightened.

Has Morton discovered I've fled, and called the police? I listen intently, half-expecting a siren to come on.

What will I tell the police? What is my name? What am I doing at this hour? What crime have I committed?

When all is quiet again, I emerge from the shrubbery,

and resume walking at a fast pace. I see an expressway off to my right, not too distant, but there is a deep gully and a high fence that will prevent my crossing over to it.

Finally I come to a service station, but it is closed. In the outdoor telephone booth, I nervously check the directory for taxi companies. I memorize the number of one, and rip open the center portion of my brassiere, into which I have sewn some change and bills. By the time I extract a dime, I have forgotten the number.

Back to the directory. I insert the dime, dial the number and say I want a cab—but the voice at the other end is not reassuring:

"Where are you?"

I am, I say, in some area called University Park, and I am using the phone at a service station. It's a Standard station.

"I don't have time for games," the voice replies, and the line goes dead.

Why, I chastise myself, hadn't I learned more about my locale? I start walking again and eventually spot a delivery truck, with *Los Angeles Times* printed on its side, parked in front of a darkened store. A young man is taking papers out of the back of the truck and stacking them at the front door of the store.

He has a beard and hair to his shoulders, wears faded well-worn denims and from all appearance might be classified as "hippie." I am greatly relieved. I feel that by his style of dress he reveals himself to be a "natural" man of natural instincts and compassion. These thoughts reassure me, for I hope he will look through my torn attire, beyond my despair, and recognize me as an individual, human being.

I move into his orbit slowly, trying not to arouse suspicion. The impersonal, cold environment of brick and mortar surrounds us—the gas station, the drugstore, the food market, all stand in eerie gloom. It is totally inexplicable, but I stumble toward this man as if he were the only other survivor of a holocaust that has spared me.

Where, I ask, are all the people around here?

"I hate this area this time of the morning," he says, showing no particular interest in me as he goes on stacking his papers.

Those bundles look heavy, I say, trying desperately to be casual, not to betray my anxiety, as I watch him.

"Each one weighs six pounds," he says.

I can think only wooden thoughts, so I refrain from saying very much of anything. He must not be scared away by my obsessive need of his help. When he finishes piling the papers, and starts back to his truck, I ask if I might ride with him to a taxi stand or a bus station.

I fear that he may balk because my dress is badly torn and stained with blood. I had scraped my arms when I fell on the Morton's patio. He looks at me without judgment, though. "I'll have to deliver my papers first," he says.

I climb up in the cab beside him. We start out and he asks where I am coming from, and when I tell him the reservation, in Arizona, he surprises me by saying his grandmother is a full-blooded Sioux. Indians often laugh about the large number of Anglos who claim "full-blooded" Indian grandmothers, but I am one Anglo not about to laugh at the young man's statement. It is too direct, too guileless, for me to doubt. I look at him as though I have been divinely directed, although the coincidence is almost too much for me to believe. I decide to say as little as possible.

After some miles and another silent inspection of my bloodied torn clothes, he eventually asks, "Did someone just put you out on the highway?"

Something like that, I respond.

"But that's terrible!" he says.

I tell him that I had asked for it, in a way.

"I know where there's a police station. I can take you there." He eyes me keenly.

I don't mind going to the police, I say, hoping he will not think I am a fugitive. But I would rather not. At this point I know I will do whatever he determines. We make a half dozen stops at luxurious food shops and drugstores. I see new housing developments that spread back to the Santa Ana mountains; we drive past the impressive new University of California in Irvine. I see a modern, sprawling "Fashion Island" shopping center, and a Medical Plaza, and again the endless rows of expensive homes.

As if he understands it is painful for me to dwell on my experience of this night, the young man turns his conversation back to his grandmother and how she influenced him to live more simply. He tells me he has a garden, grows his own vegetables. He dropped out of college, seeks inner knowledge and embraces the Indian and Oriental concept of *being* rather than doing or planning. Yet he also lives in the world of mechanistic delivery trucks.

What he says is puzzling but terribly satisfying to me, because he accepts me as a reasonably literate and intelligent person, despite my clothes and the circumstances of our encounter. He unknowingly permits me to shed the "dumb Betsy" burden imposed by the Mortons.

I had temporarily, though perhaps dangerously, lost my sense of self. I went to the Indians thinking they were "alien" and now I have come from the Mortons convinced they are "alien," the antithesis of all that I can say is my way, my people.

His easy identification with me, "Indian," has the same rejuvenating effect as my looking into a mirror and seeing myself—beautiful. All that I believe in, living simply and naturally, he expresses in his actions, his words.

He leaves me at the bus depot in Newport Beach. The station is closed, but a sign on the door says the first bus to Los Angeles leaves at 6 A.M. I calculate I must have escaped the house about three hours earlier.

Yet, have I really "escaped"? I cannot shake the idea that I am a fugitive until I get far beyond the reach of the Mortons. The Good Samaritan, with his respectful manner, has restored some of my self-confidence. Now, thrown back on my own resources, I am again oddly fearful of my "masters," half-expecting them to overtake me with a legal lien on my soul. I must expunge them from my mind and seize control of myself.

Plan tomorrow!—I barely hear the small voice. Again I feel as I did in my years with my husband Clay: I willed away my will; whatever *he* felt I must do, I somehow acted out, even when logic said no.

In the small pocket where I had sewed some money I have a couple of telephone numbers, including the number for my employer. In spite of my better counsel I find myself walking into a street phone booth and dialing the Morton number. The phone rings four times before a very sleepy Mrs. Morton picks it up. By her dull "Hullo" I know they did not hear me leave.

I tell her briefly—I didn't want you to wake up and find me gone, without some explanation. Her silence is almost wrathful. I know she's stunned. Apparently turning to her husband, she says, "It's—it's BETSY." Her tone is full of contempt. "She's *run off!*" She leaves me feeling disloyal, ungrateful, traitorous.

She again attempts to instill her will, with the voice of sweet reasonableness: "Betsy, what's wrong? What are you doing—away from home!"

I am, I tell her, going back to the reservation.

"But why, Betsy, WHY? What happened?"

It's all too different, I say.

"Why different?" Her voice now skirts the edge of hysteria.

I stand mutely, unable to answer.

"Betsy," she screams into the phone. *"How is it different?"*

I can think of no simple explanation, so I fumble for some quick words, but cannot speak them. The silence infuriates her, and she slams the phone down and leaves me aching with new fears.

Now surely they will call the police! Won't they at once check their fine silver, their jewels? If they should imagine anything missing, won't Betsy be accused? I remember only too well my experience as a "black" woman when a white Mississippi banker tried to assault me and I fled from the house, knowing that had I been arrested by white racist police they would have taken *his* word—not mine. One has only to escape his "whiteness" for five minutes to know the meaning of the old dictum: "If you're white you're right; if you're black or colored—stand back."

Agonizingly, I wait for the bus, stationing myself in an alley, to avoid the police, the Mortons, anyone seeking to block my increasingly desperate passage.

When I see the bus approaching I run, almost as if the skies were raining bombs and I were fleeing to an air raid shelter. The bus will be a haven. Away from the threatening past. But once on the bus, I try to shrink in size, somehow to make myself invisible. The bus makes several stops, but I stay aboard. The trip to Los Angeles seems an eternity.

In the terminal ladies' room—the same one where Bessie Yellowhair spent the night on a hard bench?—I splash cold water into my face. Then I retrieve from my undergarment the home number of my friend Jo. Ordinarily I might have remembered Jo's number, but lately I am forgetful of my own name.

I dial the number. Jo and I have been "best friends" since we were eighteen, but I do not know her husband so well. And it is he who answers. "Jo is out of town," he tells me. And then he adds, "And I'm leaving for Las Vegas this afternoon." With Jo gone, and Sherman her husband leaving, I feel my lifeline is slipping, perhaps disappearing.

Quickly I tell him I've been "passing" as a Navajo and that I desperately need his help. I explain I have less than five dollars in cash and no identification cards and that I am sure no hotel clerk will consider me a good credit risk.

"Where are you?" he asks.

The Greyhound station, the main one, I tell him. But would he—I ask—please hold the phone. Wait, just *wait*.

I leave the receiver dangling and walk outside, and to a corner. I must see a definite sign. I return to the phone and give him the exact street where I will be standing. When I hang up, I am uncertain what I have said. I am compelled to return to the corner, to convince myself that I know where I am.

Only when Sherman pulls up to the curb, after what seems like an eternity, am I finally persuaded that I have walked back into my own world and culture. And yet I feel no peace, no safety—not yet anyhow.

Epilogue

I wanted to go among the Indians, free of my past, an empty vessel, a clean slate, to be nothing and absorb everything, to *see, hear, understand* only that which was revealed to me.

But one can't obliterate his past, his conceptions and habits of a lifetime. So the harsh adjusting was a ceaseless struggle, while the Navajos around me had an unknowing acceptance of their lot.

I tried to understand them through an *action.* I recalled my meeting Chang in Korea and attempting through a love for him to love Korea, and I asked myself: why not "love" a Navajo? As if through that physical action, I might weigh more accurately and measure more fairly what I would learn. But who of the bleeding hearts, those who "love" the Indians, has ever come to understanding? This kind of "love" only separates people.

When I slept on dirt floors, I nagged myself constantly: these people are dirty! And when I saw their poverty, I berated them silently: why doesn't that old woman weave another rug? Why doesn't that young Navajo go out and get a job, use his back and his hands, to better himself? Why do they refuse to assimilate?

Casting aside my judgments was not required when I lived among black Americans; blacks, perhaps much more than whites, have the Judeo-Christian ethic: work hard and you succeed, and they all want the "good" things in life as we believe in the "good"—"good" hot and cold running water, "good" clothes, a "good" carpet on the floor, a "good" bed and "good" food.

Vine Deloria, Jr., the Indian authority who wrote *Custer Died for Your Sins,* says, "Indians have not yet left the Aboriginal universe in which they have always dwelled emotionally and intellectually." The words Indian and primitive must be thought of as synonymous. It is their "primitive" nature, their refusal to adapt to our work ethic, that preserved the Navajos from enslavement either by the Spaniards or the Anglos.

It wasn't long before I felt that many Navajos still retain a precious quality that I have lost: they are "connected" with all of creation. They possess, as Baudelaire phrased it, the "genius of childhood."

The primitive sees, smells, hears, tastes—with a directness of perception. Modern man, although he too feels somewhere deep within him a link to nature, has "disconnected" from creation, and busied himself with his machine civilization. Technologically we have very nearly perfected the knack of arranging the world so that we don't have to experience it.

When we move away from small primary groups, we no longer enjoy the kind of intimate relationships that are possible among primitives who live in dirt-floor huts.

One's social world enlarges; I know more people, in dozens of countries around the world, than perhaps Aunt Zonie will ever see in a lifetime. Yet, as my number of acquaintances increases, the depth of relationships decreases. I have "many friends," but the nature of urban friendships is commonly superficial, symbolized by telephone numbers and zip codes.

Because modern man no longer lives intimately, one with another, as Aunt Zonie lived with her husband, sleeping on sheepskins by the fire, he turns his lonely spirit and his lonely body more and more to other lonely bodies, with less and less intimacy and understanding.

But the flesh-against-flesh will not cure our loneliness.

Our alienation is from our "mother" earth. And to find "me" I must find myself in the totality of the universe that allows me to identify with God. Or, whatever name I give Creation-Creator.

Many students, in their "new naturalism," are seeking a recognition of the values of the Aboriginal World. They are saying: let's reject mastery over nature, let's live close to nature, in the open, off the land, stressing cooperation rather than competition. They are saying: let's place sensory experience ahead of conceptual knowledge. They are saying: it's not true we live because we consume; we don't. It's not true that we live because we are celebrated, "established"; we don't.

They reject Napoleon and Alexander as "heroes." And many are beginning to doubt that Galileo, Watt and Edison have contributed as much and as lastingly to human advancement and happiness as Socrates, Lao-tze, and Francis of Assisi.

Vine Deloria says the fate of the Aboriginal people depends upon the super nations of the world. We know the past—a long record of "civilization" linked to "violence." Short of some spiritual revolution, we will one day see the end of all primitive societies. All people will become homogenized citizens in a homogenized world.

Someone once observed that Indians are persons just like us, who also inhabit the far country of our childhood and our dreams. I went into this experience as if going backward in time. Inseparable from a journey to the Indians is a nostalgia for what is no longer and yet might have been. Yet, we cannot be cured of our industrial society and its megalomania by becoming "noble savages." Only in imagination can one go back in history.

The fate of the Navajos relates to the fate of the Aboriginal peoples, all of them, on this earth. They should be able to choose the kind of life they live.

Simple, communal life has been practiced for many centuries, among many peoples. The evidence suggests that membership in a group sustains a man, enables him to maintain his equilibrium under the ordinary shocks of life. Undoubtedly it provides many comforts and advantages. I come back to what I basically believe: that I am sovereign. No clan or cult—no government, even—and no one religion speaks for me. I am "free" to be my individual self; and for me, striving has been an end as well as a means. Struggle. Even anguish. If it had not been there, I would have felt the need to invent it.

When I first went to the reservation, I felt very much a "white" looking into the Indian world. Then in Bessie Yellowhair's clothes and her frame of mind, I momentarily became "Indian." Returning, ill from having to reconcile two worlds, I asked: who actually am I? With Ulysses, I am part of all I have met, and a part of me always will be Bessie Yellowhair.